DEVELOPING **OUTSTANDING**
PRACTICE IN
SCHOOL-BASED TEACHER EDUCATION

Critical Guides for
Teacher Educators

You might also like the following books from Critical Publishing

Developing Creative and Critical Educational Practitioners
By Victoria Door
978-1-909682-37-5
October 2014

Dial M for Mentor: Critical Reflections on Mentoring for Coaches, Educators and Trainers
By Jonathan Gravells and Susan Wallace
978-1-909330-00-9
Published 2012

How Do Expert Primary Classteachers Really Work? A Critical Guide for Teachers, Headteachers and Teacher Educators
By Tony Eaude
978-1-909330-01-6
Published 2012

Non-directive Coaching: Attitudes, Approaches and Applications
By Bob Thomson
978-1-909330-57-3
Published 2013

Theories of Professional Learning: A Critical Guide for Teacher Educators
By Carey Philpott
978-1-909682-33-7
October 2014

Most of our titles are also available in a range of electronic formats. To order please go to our website www.criticalpublishing.com or contact our distributor, NBN International, 10 Thornbury Road, Plymouth PL6 7PP, telephone 01752 202301 or email orders@nbninternational.com.

DEVELOPING **OUTSTANDING**
PRACTICE IN
SCHOOL-BASED TEACHER EDUCATION

Series Editor: **Ian Menter**

Critical Guides for
Teacher Educators

Kim **Jones**
Elizabeth **White**

First published in 2014 by Critical Publishing Ltd

British Library Cataloguing in Publication Data
A CIP record for this book is available from the British Library

ISBN: 978-1-909682-41-2

This book is also available in the following e-book formats:
MOBI ISBN: 978-1-909682-42-9
EPUB ISBN: 978-1-909682-43-6
Adobe e-book ISBN: 978-1-909682-44-3

Cover and text design by Greensplash Limited
Project Management by Out of House Publishing
Typeset by Newgen Knowledge Works
Printed and bound in Great Britain by TJ International

Critical Publishing
152 Chester Road
Northwich
CW8 4AL

www.criticalpublishing.com

CONTENTS

FOREWORD

It has become something of a cliché to say that those of us involved in teacher education 'live in interesting times'. However, such has been the rate of change in many aspects of teacher education in many parts of the world over recent years that this does actually need to be recognised. Because of the global interest in the quality of teaching and the recognition that teacher learning and development of teachers plays a crucial part in this, politicians and policymakers have shown increasing interest in the nature of teacher preparation. Early in 2013, the British Educational Research Association (BERA) in collaboration with the Royal Society for the Arts (RSA) established an inquiry into the relationship between research and teacher education. The final report from this inquiry was published in 2014 (BERA/RSA 2014) and sets out a range of findings including calling for all of those involved – policymakers, practitioners, researchers – *'to exercise leadership amongst their members and partners in promoting the use of evidence, enquiry and evaluation to prioritise the role of research and to make time and resources available for research engagement'* (p 27). One key purpose of this series of *Critical Guides for Teacher Educators* is to provide a resource that will facilitate a concerted move in this direction. The series aims to offer insights for all those with responsibilities in our field, to support their critical engagement with practice and policy through the use of evidence based on research and on experience.

In this particular volume, Kim Jones and Liz White have assembled a superb set of perspectives on the nature of what has become known as school-based teacher education. They draw on their own extensive professional experience to assess how it is that teacher education that is increasingly led from schools can retain the intellectual and professional integrity that is so important in the development of teachers in the twenty-first century. We see in England, with the promotion of schemes such as Teach First and School Direct, as well as the continuing operation of School-Centred Initial Teacher Training (SCITT), how important the deployment of critical perspectives may be. Each chapter is inspired by a key critical question and the respective authors draw on research as well as experience in addressing the issues. It is also crucial that we continue to compare and contrast our own experiences with those working in other jurisdictions and so it is extremely valuable to have chapters written from a Dutch perspective – the Netherlands is one of the nations where models of clinical practice in teacher education are being carried out on a systematic basis.

Jones and White offer us key insights for ensuring that rigour and quality are sustained as school-based staff take an increasingly central role in many aspects of teacher education. This volume should provide invaluable support for those staff as well as for those in universities who are seeking to work effectively within these new arrangements.

Ian Menter, Series Editor

Professor of Teacher Education, University of Oxford

October 2014

Ian Menter is Professor of Teacher Education and Director of Professional Programmes in the Department of Education at the University of Oxford. He previously worked at the Universities of Glasgow, the West of Scotland, London Metropolitan, the West of England and Gloucestershire. Before that he was a primary school teacher in Bristol, England. His most recent publications include *A Literature Review on Teacher Education for the 21ˢᵗ Century* (Scottish Government) and *A Guide to Practitioner Research in Education* (Sage). His work has also been published in many academic journals.

Kim Jones worked as a science teacher in Hertfordshire for 35 years. She has been on the leadership team of a secondary academy for the past 12 years. She originally became involved in teacher education as the professional mentor at this school, overseeing the training of PGCE (Postgraduate Certificate in Education) students from a number of universities. In 2004, the school joined the Alban Federation and began training teachers via an employment-based route. In 2009 she took over as ITE (Initial Teacher Education) manager for the Federation, which has since successfully become accredited as a SCITT provider (School-Centred Initial Teacher Training) and was recognised by Ofsted (Office for Standards in Education, Children's Services and Skills) as an outstanding provider in 2012.

Elizabeth White has been working in employment-based ITT (Initial Teacher Training) for the Hertfordshire Regional Partnership while being employed as a secondary science teacher. In 2009 the provision was graded as outstanding by Ofsted. She was involved in setting up the School Direct Programme in the School of Education at the University of Hertfordshire, which she now facilitates. Her research has included a self-study of her experience as a new teacher educator, developing a new aspect to her identity. She is currently researching how to effectively support school-based teacher educators in their professional development effectively.

ABOUT THE **CONTRIBUTORS**

Lynn Chapman has been working on the PGCE route into ITE for nine years. She was involved in setting up the School-Led Partnership in the School of Education at the University of Hertfordshire, which she now facilitates. Her main area of research is how to give student teachers authentic experiences in school which allow them to make the links between theory and practice and close the theory/practice divide.

Sue Field currently works in teacher education following 20 years of teaching modern foreign languages in comprehensive schools. She has taught students on PGCE and master's degree courses in the Faculty of Education at Canterbury Christ Church University. Sue was Associate Editor of the Teacher Training Resource Bank (TTRB), a highly successful government-funded website, providing reviews of resources contributing to the research and evidence base underpinning teacher education. Recently she has been a visiting lecturer at the University of Wolverhampton, and an Academic Associate for the Higher Education Academy. She is currently completing a Doctorate in Education with a focus on the pedagogy of ITE.

Amanda Roberts currently works as a senior lecturer in the School of Education at the University of Hertfordshire. Prior to this she held a range of leadership roles in secondary schools, culminating in headship. She subsequently formed and led an educational consultancy company providing support for leadership and learning in a variety of contexts including schools in challenging circumstances. Her research interests currently focus on the development of teacher educator identity.

Anja Swennen works at the VU University Amsterdam as a researcher and teacher educator. Her main research interests lie in the development of the profession and the identity of teacher educators. Anja has published several articles and books in this field, such as 'The quality of teacher educators in the European policy debate: Actions and measures to improve the professionalism of teacher educators' (Snoek et al, 2011) and 'The professional development of teacher educators' (a special issue of *Professional Development in Education*, published as a book by Routledge, 2011).

Miranda Timmermans studied developmental psychology, has a special interest in social constructivism and competence-oriented teacher training and has worked in teacher education for 20 years. Her thesis on school-based teacher training focused on the quality of the teaching schools in which student teachers are placed. Her research resulted in a validated, developmentally oriented self-assessment instrument for teaching schools. Miranda has recently been working at the Netherlands Association of Universities of Applied Sciences as a project manager developing national assessments of student teachers' knowledge.

Corrine van Velzen started as a teacher educator focusing on the development of science teaching. From 1990 she worked in higher education in Social and Community Work preparing students to teach children and adults in settings other than school. Having started at VU University in 1999 she is involved in higher and secondary education and in the development of school/university partnerships. Her main research focus is the development of work-based teacher education and the development of teachers as teacher educators.

ACKNOWLEDGEMENTS

This book has been written to help teachers and teacher educators who are leading the professional development of a new generation of teachers within their schools and higher education institutions. We would like to thank all the teachers and teacher educators who have contributed to our research directly and those who have influenced us while we have been working collaboratively on initial and continuing professional development programmes. Our thanks go to Julia Morris at Critical Publishing, and her colleagues, for their guidance in the production of this book. We hope that you will be stimulated in your thinking as you develop your professional practice both personally and within and between your institutions.

ABBREVIATIONS

ATEE	Association for Teacher Education in Europe
BERA	British Educational Research Association
DfE	Department for Education
HEA	Higher Education Academy
HEI	Higher Education Institution
IBTE	Institute-Based Teacher Educator
ITE	Initial Teacher Education
NCTL	National College for Teaching and Learning
NQT	Newly Qualified Teacher
Ofsted	Office for Standards in Education, Children's Services and Skills
PGCE	Postgraduate Certificate in Education
QA	Quality Assurance
QTS	Qualified Teacher Status
SBTE	School-Based Teacher Educator
SCITT	School-Centred Initial Teacher Training
TEI	Teacher Education Institute
UCET	Universities Council for the Education of Teachers
VELON	Association of Dutch Teacher Educators

Kim Jones and Liz White

CRITICAL **ISSUES**

- *Setting the scene: the current context in ITE*
- *Personal challenges for teacher educators*
- *Learning from different models*

Introduction

Teacher education is in a state of dynamic flux across the United Kingdom and internationally. Many teachers are taking on teacher education roles in schools, colleges and universities for the first time. There is a need to provide high-quality, relevant and rigorous ITE in order to develop committed professionals who are able to offer the best possible learning experiences for all pupils in this and future generations.

Across many Western countries there is a growth of government policies which are designed to promote more school-led models of teacher education. In England, the government-driven changes are probably more radical than those being experienced in other countries. These changes were announced in *The Importance of Teaching: Schools White Paper* (DfE, 2010). A new emphasis on outstanding schools leading the training and professional development of teachers was heralded, through the designation of 'teaching schools'. The initial plans were developed further (DfE, 2011), building on the premise that teachers in schools are the best people to be leading teacher education. The following statement is included in the vision and background to teaching schools on the NCTL (National College for Teaching and Learning) website.

Teaching schools will play a fundamental role in developing a self-sustaining system where:

- *trainee teachers learn from the best teachers, supported by a culture of coaching and mentoring;*
- *professional development is school-based and classroom focused – teachers, support staff and leaders improve through exposure to excellent practice within and beyond their immediate school, through observation, mentoring, coaching, practice, reflection and sharing with peers.*

(DfE, 2012a)

The first step the government has taken toward achieving this in England has been the introduction of the School Direct programme, which is described as:

part of a wider set of reforms designed to help schools take greater responsibility for leading and shaping Initial Teacher Training, including new approaches to university-school partnerships, Teaching Schools' Initial Teacher Training role, and the accreditation of new school-led providers.

(Teaching Agency, 2012)

As a result, the relationship between schools and accredited providers such as Higher Education Institutions (HEIs) and School-Centred Initial Teacher Training providers (SCITTs) is rapidly changing.

Critical questions

» Where is teacher education located and who leads it in your context?

» What are the challenges in your national context?

Teacher educators

Teacher educators facilitate the professional development of teachers by providing learning opportunities through a variety of means and in a range of contexts. The teachers may be at any stage of their career; however, within this book we are focusing on nurturing student teachers and NQTs (Newly Qualified Teachers) in particular. Because of the changing terrain, there is increased diversification of teacher educators as an occupational group. Many ITE programmes are situated in HEIs, with institute-based teacher educators (IBTEs) who have strong academic backgrounds facilitating the learning (Chapter 2, Swennen, and Chapter 8, van Velzen and Timmermans). Experienced teachers in schools may work as school-based teacher educators (SBTEs), supporting the learning of student teachers and NQTs in the classroom by taking on roles as mentors or tutors (Chapter 6, Chapman, and Chapter 7, Jones). Others are *hybrid educators* (Zeichner, 2010) who work in both settings. In the Netherlands, teachers who are involved in ITE are known as cooperating teachers. Within this group the term SBTE is used for those with more of an overseeing role in school, rather than the teacher (or daily) mentor who works alongside the student teacher from day to day (Chapter 8, van Velzen and Timmermans). In England the term professional mentor is commonly used for this role (Chapter 7, Jones). In summary, there is a diverse group of individuals whom we would view as having this privileged role of being teacher educators. With the current rapid rate of change there are challenges for all teacher educators in terms of their roles and responsibilities and their professional identities, within whichever context they are working.

Training or education?

A debate surrounds the nature of the preparation of teachers with a number of national governments promoting the concept of ITE as training, implying that teaching is a set of skills that student teachers can learn through apprenticeship without associated academic underpinning. While learning teaching does include acquiring a range of classroom and behaviour-management skills, it is our belief that this alone does not develop outstanding teachers who enable pupils to fulfil both their academic and personal potential. Rather, there is a need to develop student teachers as reflective practitioners who can adjust their teaching approaches to meet the needs of learners because they have a critical and rigorous approach and a growing understanding of:

» the theories of learning;

» their own subject(s);

» the context and culture in which they work locally and nationally.

This is more than just training in the skills of teaching; this is the all-encompassing scope of education. Teacher education is the remit of teacher educators who are cultivating an identity beyond that of a teacher of children (Chapter 2, Swennen). The role of a teacher educator could be seen as being an 'enriched' teacher, requiring additional skills, knowledge and pedagogical approaches. The challenges of developing an effective pedagogy for teaching about teaching are deliberated in Chapter 3. In Chapter 4 the concept of developing an academic identity through practice-based research and scholarship is considered in a way that is relevant to all teacher educators. These are some of the personal challenges of educating a new generation of teachers that will be considered in Part A of the book.

As many teachers are taking on the new role of teacher educator in their own settings, there is an urgent need to develop a community of practitioners where their needs can be met, enabling them to consider the challenges of this work alongside those with more experience. This may be especially demanding while continuing their prime role as teacher and remaining in the context where their teacher identity is well established and the overarching priority is the education of children rather than the education of teachers.

Critical questions

» What personal challenges do you face in your role in teacher education?

» How will you balance this against the expectation to consistently deliver outstanding classroom teaching and the high demands this, in itself, makes?

» What do you believe the role of a teacher educator should encompass?

» How can you engage with a community of teacher educators where your identity, knowledge and practice can be strengthened?

Recently, Davey has explored the professional identity of teacher educators in *Career on the Cusp?* (Davey, 2013). This volume draws on the findings of the author's research, revealing issues that are real for new and developing IBTEs in their professional role, context and identity. Although in a different context to SBTEs there are many common elements around the challenges and opportunities that arise from constantly evolving education policies.

Different models of teacher education

Leading teacher education takes us beyond our personal development in this role and into the domain of what institutional models we can develop to best meet the needs of the new generation of teachers alongside whom we are working. This is explored in Part B of the book. What is meant by outstanding provision is debated in Chapter 5, drawing out some themes that are illustrated in the rest of the book:

> » having an inquiry-based approach;
>
> » building a learning community;
>
> » developing reflective practitioners;
>
> » having an ethos of high aspiration;
>
> » evaluating the impact of the programme on the quality of teaching.

The opportunity to consider developments in England and in the Netherlands has provided much food for thought. Chapter 6 describes a partnership model used in England to develop a series of school-led modules that help to integrate theory and practice. The impact of this approach was evaluated on both the outcomes for student teachers and their ability to link theory and practice.

The development of a learning community in a partnership of secondary schools in England is illustrated in Chapter 7. From this SCITT model we also see how student teachers are developed into reflective practitioners, how an ethos of high aspiration is maintained across the partnership and how the impact of the ITE is evaluated.

Finally, in Chapter 8 a school-centred model for ITE in the Netherlands demonstrates how practice-based inquiry aimed at improving the practice of student teachers and school development is part of the curriculum of ITE.

Critical questions

> » What underpinning theory and research is necessary for an effective new generation of teachers?
>
> » How can you develop post-graduate thinking in your developing teachers?
>
> » In what ways do you nurture your partnerships?

IN A **NUTSHELL**

This book is designed to stimulate thinking and discussion rather than provide definitive answers. We present models as useful case studies rather than a comprehensive review of ITE. Our intention is to help teacher educators to develop their professional practice both personally and across their institutions. We hope you will be provoked into moving your practice forward and becoming the best teacher educator that you can be for your emergent teachers, whether you are part of the growing group of SBTEs or based in an institute, and whether you are new to this role or experienced. We believe that the individual roles of teacher educators must be supported by leaders of ITE who have a clear concept of what outstanding provision looks like and how to achieve it. Reflecting on a variety of institutional models provides a stimulus for this discussion.

REFLECTIONS ON **CRITICAL ISSUES**

- *Taking on the role of a teacher educator involves developing a new aspect to your professional identity, as well as requiring the development of new understanding and skills. Current shifts towards school-led provision are opening opportunities for more teachers to be involved in ITE while continuing their primary roles as teachers and while working within their school context.*

- *National and local policies can:*

    - *change the context in which we work to nurture a new generation of teachers;*

    - *provide challenges to the sustainability and quality of teacher education;*

    - *offer opportunities to develop new approaches that build on the current strengths of using the workplace as a learning environment.*

- *Examining different models of leading school-based teacher education can afford insights for emergent routes into teaching.*

Part A

Personal challenges

CHAPTER 2 | MORE THAN JUST A TEACHER: THE IDENTITY OF TEACHER EDUCATORS

Anja Swennen

CRITICAL **ISSUES**

- *Who are teacher educators?*
- *What are the identities of teacher educators in institutes and schools?*
- *How do teachers develop as teacher educators?*

Introduction

When I became a primary teacher educator in the Netherlands, neither the head of the teacher education institute (TEI) nor my colleagues considered interfering with the contents of my teaching, let alone with how I should teach – and frankly I did not expect this either at the time. The assumption was that because I had prior experience in secondary and higher education I would be adept at teacher education. Most of the other teacher educators had been primary school teachers and had studied for a subject degree. We thought about ourselves as teachers in teacher education but not as teacher educators and this term was not used by any of us until years later.

While teacher education is strongly rooted in the historical, cultural and economic context of nations, I am sure that teacher educators from different parts of Europe recognise my early experiences. Many newly appointed teacher educators may state that their own induction phase was not that different from the one teachers experienced 25 years ago (van Velzen et al, 2010). In this chapter I describe how the professional identity of teacher educators has changed over the past 25 years from that of teacher in teacher education to the complex professional identity in the contemporary context. I will draw on a range of sources including my recent research embracing the development of primary teacher education in the Netherlands and the professional life histories of five teacher educators of different generations working from 1960 until now (Swennen, 2012).

Critical questions

- » What has been your journey into teacher education?
- » Do you see yourself as a teacher educator or as a teacher working in teacher education?

Identity of teacher educators

The concept of professional identity is complex (Beauchamp and Thomas, 2009) and the meaning differs both between and within various disciplines. The identity of teacher educators develops within the social and cultural context in which they:

> » grow up (such as their family);

> » are educated (like the schools they attend);

> » work (for example schools and institutes).

The identity of teachers is the outcome of their past experience (Beijaard et al, 2004) and the development of their professional identity starts with childhood observations of their teachers, with whom they may or may not identify (Zeichner and Gore, 1990). The identity of teacher educators is additionally influenced by their personal interpretation of prior experience. Views on the profession and the identity of teachers are also shaped by previous generations of teacher educators and others who have influenced education, including researchers and politicians. Teacher educators who join the profession have to relate to existing traditions, customs and written and unwritten rules of the profession (Penuel and Wertsch, 1995) and build their own identity as a teacher educator.

Studying the development of the identity of teachers and teacher educators assumes that professional identity is changeable and changing (Beijaard et al, 2004). People have a certain degree of control, or agency, over their identity and the development of that identity. Agency gives a degree of control not only over the development of an individual's personal and professional identity but, according to Hermans and Hermans-Konopka (2010), also over developments and innovations in one's work.

Critical question

> » Can you identify influences in your past that have shaped your identity as a teacher educator?

Not all teachers are teacher educators

After several years in primary teacher education I joined the Association of Dutch Teacher Educators (VELON) and the Association for Teacher Education in Europe (ATEE). I discovered there was more to educating teachers than being a good teacher yourself and that those in this role were called teacher educators. Becoming involved in research made me aware that there are different ways to define teacher educators and that these depend on the national, cultural and personal views of researchers and practitioners. Some state that every teacher is a teacher educator as they show, in a positive or less positive way, what teachers are and do, and as such all teachers are models for future teachers. This is a popular definition in policy documents where it is argued, for more economic than idealistic reasons, that all teachers can educate future teachers. For the purpose of this chapter this definition is too wide. For me, teacher educators are those who contribute formally to the education of teachers in pre-service and in-service education. This means that SBTEs and those leading in-service education are regarded as teacher educators in the same way as traditional teacher educators who work for institutes.

Fisher (2009) defines teacher educators by the work they do and, more specifically, by the standards for teacher educators. These have been developed by the Association of Teacher Education in the United States and also by VELON, and not by governments, and are used by teacher educators to improve the quality of their individual work and that of the profession. The Dutch standards for teacher educators are evolving and adapting to the ever-changing work of teacher educators.

In these standards there are four competencies for teacher educators and, within each of these, several sub-categories. Teacher educators have to be able to:

1. educate teachers (explicit modelling is a sub-category);
2. work with adults (working with a diverse population of student teachers is a sub-category);
3. organise (working in a multidisciplinary team is a sub-category);
4. professionally develop themselves (being a reflective practitioner is a sub-category).

In addition, five specific roles of teacher educators are described: (i) subject pedagogy educator, (ii) curriculum developer, (iii) assessor, (iv) in-service educator and (v) researcher (see: http://www.velon.nl/beroepsstandaard). This suggests that teacher educators are involved in different sorts of professional activities and enact a variety of roles.

While the above definitions may be useful, they do not quite define what characterises teacher educators and how they are different from school teachers or lecturers in higher education. Murray suggested the notion of teacher educators as second-order practitioners (Murray, 2002) to distinguish between the work of teachers, as first-order teaching, and the work of teacher educators, as second-order teaching. Teachers teach in a first-order situation: they teach their subject to their pupils. Their professional knowledge is for the greater part tacit and cannot easily be made explicit. Moreover this knowledge is closely connected to practice and to the individual views of teachers about teaching and learning. Teacher educators distinguish themselves from teachers because they are practising 'second-order teaching': '*As second-order practitioners teacher educators induct their student teachers into the practices and discourses of both school teaching and teacher education*' (Murray and Male, 2005, p 126). This notion of teacher educators as first-order and second-order practitioners not only adds important terms to the language of teacher education, but also helps us to think about the identity, the work and the different positions of teacher educators who work for institutes from those who work for schools.

Critical questions

» How would you define the different aspects of your role as a teacher educator?

» What do you see as the benefits and drawbacks of having professional standards for teacher educators?

But all teacher educators are teachers

Being a teacher is at the very core of the identity of teacher educators. Many IBTEs were previously teachers in schools and now educate student teachers. Educating here encompasses all activities of the work of teacher educators, like teaching small or large groups, and supervising the school practice and research of student teachers. An important characteristic of IBTEs is that at some point in their careers they decided to leave primary or secondary education to work in teacher education.

Klecka et al (2008) suggest that the identity of the teacher that the IBTE once was remains strong throughout their career. Teacher educators cherish their identity as a teacher for several reasons:

» they gain confidence from their former identity as teachers during the sometimes difficult early years as teacher educators (Swennen et al, 2009);

» it can be a relief for teacher educators to experience that teaching student teachers is not so different from teaching pupils in schools (Kosnik, 2007);

» their previous experience makes them credible in the eyes of the student teachers and mentors (Dinkelman et al, 2006).

The previous identity of teachers is not only appreciated by themselves, their student teachers and mentors, but also by managers and policy developers. However, the identity of the teacher belongs to the professional past of the IBTE. Most researchers studying teacher educators emphasise that someone who is a good teacher is not necessarily a good teacher educator (Loughran, 2006; Zeichner, 2005a). Teacher educators should be able to use their experience as a first-order teacher:

» to reflect on their own teaching ('is this helpful for my student teachers?');

» to reflect on good teaching in general;

» to help their student teachers to reflect on their teaching (Chapter 5, White and Jones, and Chapter 7, Jones).

Cochran-Smith (2003) observes that teacher educators may be uncomfortable with the label of teacher educator and do not always identify with being teachers of teachers: '*the identity of these professors is closely linked to subject matter areas such as mathematics or composition, to specialty areas such as early childhood or learning disabilities, and/or to the disciplines generally housed within schools and colleges of education such as psychology or testing and measurement*' (Cochran-Smith, 2003, p 22). My recent research (Swennen,

2012) confirms these findings. When they were working as teachers, the teacher educators studied for their teaching degree, a non-academic degree for secondary education, for about five years to raise their professional status. By doing this they consolidated their identity as subject teachers which they maintained and valued throughout their careers. The teacher educators I studied did not call themselves teacher educator – one even resented the name – but they identified with being subject teachers, subject pedagogy teachers and lecturers in higher education.

Critical question

» How does your identity as a teacher inform your practice as a teacher educator?

Some are lecturers in higher education

In the 1990s teacher education moved from being in relatively independent colleges to being part of higher education. Currently in some European countries the TEI is part of a research university, in others it is situated in a university of applied science, or in some countries both. Teacher education has become increasingly professional and, as a result, the heads of TEIs and governments favour recent and relevant experience and appoint school teachers as teacher educators (Harrison and McKeon, 2008). Teacher educators usually have a master's degree while school teachers have a bachelor's degree and a strong identity as a teacher.

All school teachers who start working as teacher educators in institutes have to develop an identity as a lecturer in higher education (Murray and Male, 2005). Developing this identity means teachers have to adapt to teaching adults who want to become teachers. They also have to adapt to using the pedagogies of higher education like:

» competence-based education;
» problem-based education;
» practice-based education.

Additionally, they have to adapt to tasks that differ from traditional school teaching like working in a larger and more complex organisation (Swennen et al, 2009). They also have to learn how to collaborate with their former colleagues in school who are mentoring student teachers.

While some are school-based teacher educators and mentors

For me, one of the aspects of being a teacher educator was visiting a variety of schools. When there was time I discussed the progress with the mentor, but if not I just talked with the student teacher about their lesson preparation and observed their teaching. The role of the mentor was limited and rather passive. With the professionalisation of teacher education the contribution of schools and mentors was, and still is, increasing. Teaching schools are now in place, and educating teachers is often a joint partnership between schools and institutes (see for example White, 2014). As a result school teachers who supervise student teachers now increasingly play a formal role in the education of teachers and as such are regarded as SBTEs (Chapter 8, van Velzen and Timmermans).

SBTEs continue to work as first-order practitioners. Usually their main identity remains that of teacher. In their role as SBTEs, their position can be characterised as being second-order practitioners in a first-order context. This position may explain why student teachers value the advice and guidance of SBTEs or mentors over that of the IBTEs. The SBTEs are 'real' teachers but they are not, or at least should not be, 'just' teachers. Perhaps, more than IBTEs, mentors can use their everyday experience as teachers to support the learning of their future colleagues (van Velzen et al, 2012).

Teacher educators as researchers?

It must be evident by now that, when I started, teacher educators were not involved in research activities. It was not uncommon though for teacher educators, back then and now, to publish articles in teacher education journals and write textbooks. By doing this they read existing literature and developed their writing skills and could be considered as *consumers of research* (Cochran-Smith, 2005). The move into higher education, and the attempt to increase the scholarship of teacher education, now asks for IBTEs and SBTEs to develop a research identity (Murray et al, 2009).

The research of teacher educators is often regarded by themselves and others as a form of professional development, a means to improve teacher education and a way to increase the scholarship of teacher education (Cochran-Smith, 2005; Chapter 4, Roberts). However, it is generally not regarded as a contribution to the academic knowledge base of teacher education (Swennen, 2012). This may be because the academic work of teacher educators, like the research of teachers (Zeichner, 1995), is not cited as much as that of traditional academic educational researchers.

Good teachers need good teacher educators

To improve teacher education it is important to strengthen the recognition of it as a profession. The development of an identity as a teacher educator, and the skills that go with it, is a lengthy and often difficult process (Kosnik, 2007; Zeichner, 2005b). The study of Murray and Male (2005) shows that teacher educators in England need two to three years to acquire their new identity. The biggest problems they experience are developing research skills and their own pedagogy of teacher education. Induction of teacher educators and further professional opportunities for them to develop an identity as second-order practitioners and researchers are emerging, and hopefully these will evolve over the next ten years (Murray et al, 2009; White et al, 2013).

Critical question

» How will you plan for your professional learning and development as a teacher educator?

IN A **NUTSHELL**

The identity of teacher educators is complex, as shown by the various standards for teacher educators. They can be characterised as second-order practitioners. Teacher educators often have a strong identity as teachers, subject teachers and subject pedagogy teachers. Those working in an institute also develop an identity as a lecturer in higher education. More recently teacher educators are engaging in practice-based research and as such are in the process of developing a research identity. There are only a few initiatives to support teacher educators to develop an identity as teachers of teachers and as researchers.

REFLECTIONS ON **CRITICAL ISSUES**

- *Good teachers are shaped by good teacher educators.*

- *Teacher educators should be able to use their identity as school teachers as a means to reflect on their own work and that of their student teachers.*

- *Teacher educators have to develop their professional identity as teachers of teachers to enable them to develop pedagogies for teacher education.*

- *More recently the need to engage in practice-based research and develop an identity as a researcher has been added to this role.*

- *More professional development is needed for teacher educators.*

CHAPTER 3 | HOW CAN I DEVELOP OUTSTANDING TEACHERS?

Sue Field

CRITICAL ISSUES

- *In what ways does teaching differ from teaching about teaching (meta-teaching)?*
- *What adds to the complexity of meta-teaching?*
- *How might the pedagogy of teacher education contribute to the development of outstanding teachers?*

Introduction

Many teacher educators will have already experienced successful and lengthy careers as teachers in schools, and are likely to be effective classroom practitioners with curriculum subject expertise. In becoming teacher educators, pedagogy is therefore seen to be an area where they are expert and tacit assumptions appear to be made about the ease of transferring teaching skills and knowledge from a 'first-order' to a 'second-order' context (Murray and Male, 2005; Chapter 2, Swennen). This perception fails to acknowledge not only the differences between adult and young learners, but also the distinctive demands of meta-teaching (teaching about teaching). Teacher educators are required to think beyond their knowledge of how they teach their subject(s), to how they can 'teach how to teach' this to others – the desired outcome being that others will 'learn how to teach' (Field, 2012). This chapter will explore the current knowledge base for a pedagogy of teacher education and how this may inform practice that can contribute to developing outstanding teachers.

Critical question

» Can you recognise different pedagogies that you use as a teacher and as a teacher educator?

The nature of teacher education

At a fundamental level, it could be argued that there are two key questions for teacher educators in determining their pedagogy of teacher education:

1. *What are the essential qualities of a good teacher?*

2. *How can we help people to become good teachers?*

(Korthagen, 2004, p 77)

Although experienced teachers may feel confident about their teaching competence as new teacher educators, they also need to understand the subtle and intricate differences between teaching and meta-teaching. Berry (2009, p 306) goes so far as to suggest that their role *'demands a focus on knowledge about, and learning of, teaching in new and different ways such that expertise as a teacher can in fact have limited applicability in practice as a teacher educator'*. This not only means that teacher educators have to learn new pedagogical knowledge and practice, but also *un*learn well-rooted ideas, beliefs and practices (Cochran-Smith, 2003) by way of exploring their prior assumptions about teaching and learning.

There may be an initial temptation to teach and 'preach' teaching as they have taught – successfully – in school. This runs the risk of a pedagogical repertoire consisting mainly of simplistic modelling, anecdotes, and transmission (in other words, 'do as I do', 'do as I did', 'do as I say', and even 'do as I say, *not* as I do') (Field, 2012). While understandable as a response this could be seen as an impoverished pedagogical model which fails to acknowledge the 'messiness' of teaching and learning. Student teachers may recognise what and how to teach, but not why. In itself, it has the potential to do little more than clone the next generation of teachers, in much the same way as the 'sitting by Nellie' apprenticeship model of learning to teach has done in the past.

For teacher educators to move beyond this it is necessary for them first of all to recognise teaching and learning as their 'subject' content. This would contrast with teachers' knowledge and understanding of how pupils learn curriculum subjects. The knowledge needed for learning to teach can be seen to include the following:

- *personal knowledge and interpretation of experience;*
- *tacit knowledge* (instinctive knowledge)
- *process knowledge* (how we teach – general pedagogy);
- *propositional knowledge* (what we teach and the rationale for doing so);
- *theoretical knowledge of learning and teaching children;*
- *subject content and* (subject) *pedagogical knowledge.*

(Taylor, 2008, p 68)

The difference, therefore, between being a good teacher and being a good teacher educator needs to be acknowledged, which may position the teacher educator initially as the *'expert becomes novice'* (Murray, 2006, p 3).

Critical questions

» What are the essential qualities of an effective teacher? Why?

» How can we help people to become effective teachers?

Four issues impacting on the pedagogy of teacher education

The lack of a knowledge base

Teacher education is acknowledged as an under-researched and under-theorised field which lacks a coherent and specialised body of knowledge and common understanding. Even within the limited literature the focus tends to be on content and not on process; that is, on what student teachers should know, rather than on how they might learn/be taught. Rather than a *'signature pedagogy'* for teacher education (Shulman, 2005), there appears to be a plethora of visions of what it should be, as well as individual interpretations of 'what works'. Views concerning what the knowledge base for meta-pedagogy (how teaching about teaching is enacted) might be will vary according to perspectives on the intended goals and purposes of teacher education. Therefore it is useful for new teacher educators to explore their belief systems and how these impact upon their pedagogical practice as a teacher – as well as a teacher educator. The critical questions above are a good starting point although the question 'why?' also needs to be explored.

Learning to teach: the student teacher perspective

Whatever the student teachers' (or your own) background, they will need to be introduced to the current methods and practices for effectively teaching pupils. The notion that student teachers may have unrealistic expectations and beliefs about learning to teach, and somewhat fixed ideas about teaching itself, can in part be attributed to *'their apprenticeship of observation'* (Lortie, 1975). Their extensive experience as learners would have exposed them to the apparently calm surface of effective teaching which does not reveal the turbulent nature of what lies beneath. It is vital for teacher educators to create opportunities for student teachers to *'critically and objectively evaluate and understand their own internalized belief systems regarding the nature of learning that most likely have been acquired during their own schooling, when much of their learning may have been driven by more traditional forms of pedagogy'* (Fisher et al, 2010, p 94). These discussions can also lead to student teachers being encouraged to try out new practices in their own teaching, which in turn demands a continuing dialogue (Jarvis and White, 2013).

The dual role

One of the inherent causes of complexity in teacher education pedagogy lies within the notion of 'layers', reflected in this chapter in the choice of the terms 'meta-teaching' and 'meta-pedagogy'. What this means is that teacher educators are required to teach their student teachers about teaching, while also being models of teaching; that is, they are *'teaching about teaching through teaching'* (Field, 2012, p 814). This separates teacher education from other professions as well as from school teaching. For teacher educators based in school this complexity is compounded by the overlap between the newer role and activity enacted in the established role. Distinctions may need to be drawn – including to themselves – between teaching pupils and modelling teaching to student teachers (Jarvis,

2013). They need to be particularly aware of '*different levels of objective*' (Boyd and Harris, 2010, p 17) within their meta-pedagogical practice.

The theory/practice divide

Reconciling the perceived gap between theory and practice is recognised as a problem in teacher education. Traditionally the teacher educator is required to provide the knowledge of public theory, which the student teacher is expected to translate into practice, or procedural knowledge, in the classroom. Research indicates that courses where '*theory is presented without much connection to practice*' (Korthagen et al, 2005, p 107) appear to have little impact on student teachers' teaching. In the teacher educator's classroom, these connections can be made through explicit modelling, personal inquiry and investigation. Reflection and post-observation discussions during school-based experience may also '*support student teachers*' *making sense of theoretical knowledge in their professional learning*' (Cheng et al, 2012, p 783).

Any concerns that SBTEs may harbour about linking with the research agenda need to be addressed, as the role demands a secure knowledge of theory relating to teaching and learning (Chapter 4 by Amanda Roberts provides some insights into developing this knowledge). Their practical wisdom as school teachers is recognised as an important foundation for their role as a teacher educator and, in this role, they may accumulate further knowledge precisely through experiencing meta-teaching.

Critical questions

» In what ways can you raise your student teachers' awareness of their perceptions to make them available for challenge?

» How do you enact and articulate your pedagogy?

A constructivist approach to the pedagogy of teacher education

In order to develop into outstanding teachers, student teachers need to be encouraged to discover 'the teacher within themselves', rather than simply be told or shown how to be a teacher. Student teachers may crave 'tips for teachers', but unless they are able to '*understand themselves as teachers*' (Kane, 2003, p 372), they can only replicate, rather than generate, pedagogical practice. Some of the current good practice in schools is underpinned by social constructivism which recognises the prior knowledge and experience that learners bring with them and builds on this in a collaborative and discursive manner. Reflecting on this means that effective meta-pedagogical practice by the teacher educator will utilise group discussion and embrace a dialogue within which student teachers can '*construct new meaning, understand their own learning and their psychology of being a teacher*' (Fisher et al, 2010, p 95).

Personal inquiry and investigation

Through meta-pedagogies of personal inquiry and investigation student teachers can 'attend to theory in a way that is situated in practice' (Lampert, 2010, p 25). In addition to experiential learning student teachers may also experience aspects of teaching in a more clinical environment where the teacher education classroom acts as a laboratory for them to hone practice in the form of 'micro-teaching'. To support the student teachers' development the meta-pedagogy needs to comprise 'deep conversations about teaching; professionally constructed learning experiences; and non-judgemental feedback that is focussed on the use of evidence for teaching' (Ure, 2010, p 472). A similar process will surround analysis of practice from either lesson observations or from video-recorded teaching, within a learning conversation between the student teacher and the SBTE.

Reflection

An emphasis on fostering student teachers' reflection has been the main pedagogical response to closing the gap between theory and practice. This iterative process involves them enhancing their understandings of their professional practice and questioning routine situations (Berry, 2009). A range of pedagogical strategies that have been used with student teachers to promote reflection are provided by Cheng et al (2012). These include reflective tasks, video-recorded case studies, portfolios and seminars, in which teacher educators work with student teachers to examine practice in the light of theoretical inputs. In order to support reflective practice, teacher educators need to demonstrate a clear understanding of the complexities of teaching and learning as first- and second-order practitioners. While reflection is something that needs to be learnt, teacher educators must reflect on their own teaching while also enabling student teachers to be reflective, which again highlights the duality of the role (Chapter 5, White and Jones).

Explicit modelling

A central component of pedagogical practice is modelling, through which teacher behaviour (e.g. professionalism and self-reflection) and teaching behaviours (e.g. classroom routines and activities) are demonstrated to student teachers. To model good practice may be instinctive on the part of the teacher educator but needs to be made explicit to be an effective teaching method; otherwise student teachers may not learn from it as they fail to recognise it as such (Jarvis and White, 2013).

By being helped to focus and reflect through explicit modelling, student teachers can develop their own teaching. Swennen et al (2008) refer to this as 'congruent teaching', three important aspects of which are:

1. modelling;
2. explaining the choices while teaching (meta-commentary);
3. linking the choices to the relevant theory.

This involves teacher educators making explicit the tacit knowledge they accumulated as teachers, which may initially be challenging for them and could in part explain why van

Velzen's study (2013) found no evidence of explicit modelling from SBTEs. This can open up the experienced professional's practice to scrutiny and discussion in a way which may not have occurred since they were student teachers themselves. It can also allow the student teachers to see into the teacher educator's '*thinking about teaching so that they can access the ideas and feelings associated with taking risks and learning about teaching in meaningful ways*' (Korthagen et al, 2006, p 1037).

From this, it can be seen that explicit modelling has the potential to be a key component of meta-pedagogy. Literature suggests that explicit modelling does have an impact on student teachers' learning (Loughran, 2006), whereas implicit modelling remains latent and potentially of little discernible value.

Critical question

» How can you provide further opportunities for personal inquiry, reflection and explicit modelling of good practice within your context?

IN A **NUTSHELL**

When teachers become teacher educators there are assumptions made about the ease of transferring their pedagogical skills and knowledge to their new role. It should be acknowledged that there are a number of issues which make the task of developing outstanding teachers more complex, including:

» the distinctive nature of *meta*-teaching;

» a lack of common understanding about meta-pedagogy;

» the *apprenticeship of observation* and prior assumptions;

» bridging the divide between theory and practice.

In order to avoid simply cloning the next generation of teachers through modelling and transmission of what may possibly be fossilised practices, it is necessary to embrace the notion of facilitating and guiding student teachers' individual growth as teachers through their meta-pedagogical approach. This will include pedagogies of personal inquiry, investigation and reflection, as well as explicit modelling of practice.

REFLECTIONS ON **CRITICAL ISSUES**

• *In the move from first- to second-order practitioners, teacher educators need to develop and extend their pedagogical skills and repertoire as there are fundamental differences between teaching and meta-teaching.*

- *Recognising and acknowledging the complexity and demands of meta-pedagogy and of the role of the teacher educator is an important first step in developing practice.*

- *Relinquishing control in the teacher educator's classroom and accepting that facilitation and guidance are more powerful than 'telling and showing' allows the space for student teachers to develop into outstanding teachers.*

Amanda Roberts

CRITICAL **ISSUES**

- *What is meant by 'an academic identity'?*
- *How might an academic identity sit with a school teacher's identity?*
- *What is the rationale for the development of an academic aspect to a teacher's identity?*
- *How do academic identities evolve and how can they be proactively developed?*

Do I need an academic identity?

This question may, not so long ago, have seemed irrelevant to those experienced school teachers whose role included the support of student teachers and newly qualified colleagues. Its relevance may even have been challenged in Schools of Education in some universities, where a focus on the training element of preparing students for a teaching career outweighed the need for teacher educators to develop their own academic profile. A number of shifts in policy and practice have now rendered the question vitally important for all teacher educators to consider, whatever their working context.

The majority of teacher educators in universities enter Schools of Education to pursue a second career, having spent many years as school teachers. As experienced professionals, these new teacher educators bring with them a clear identity as a teacher built on previous success in supporting the learning of young people. They are often unnerved by the move to higher education (Maguire, 2000), where the organisational structures, rhythms of work and professional expectations seem alien to them. One of these alien features is the expectation that teacher educators will embrace all aspects of their academic role, including undertaking research and publication. It is unsurprising that new teacher educators typically prefer to hold on to their previously established identity as a teacher (ESRC, 2006). In a sector in which research and publication is increasingly becoming the norm, such a stance can result in these professionals being in danger of becoming '*semi-academics*' (Ducharme, 1993) who in reality only partially fulfil the expectations of their new role.

Colleagues carrying out their teacher educator role in a school context face similar and perhaps even greater challenges to their practice and identity. Some ITE programmes now attract master's-level credits, based on the requirement for aspiring teachers to undertake research. This arises from the growing body of studies that demonstrate that when teachers take an 'inquiry stance' with their practice, pupils' achievement can be raised (Cochran-Smith and Lytle, 2009; Timperley et al, 2007). Teacher educators are now expected to guide both the development of student teachers' classroom practice and their research activity, so the need to re-evaluate their own position in terms of the research and writing aspect of the teacher educators' role seems unavoidable.

It appears that an easy, agreed answer to the question posed in the title of this chapter is unlikely. It may well now be necessary for teacher educators in diverse contexts to develop their academic identity and practice in order to ensure that they fully prepare students for the wide-ranging expectations around the role of the teacher. However, individuals will rightly take their own position with regard to the question. This chapter seeks to support teacher educators in developing an authentic, personal response to this question.

What do we mean by an academic identity?

The complexity of the concept of identity makes it difficult to meaningfully define in a few words. In everyday parlance the term identity is used to reference particular characteristics and attributes of an individual. A dominant feature of this way of seeing identity is that it is fixed and inflexible. We know who we are, we know what sort of person another is (Jenkins, 1996). In this chapter I am suggesting that identity is really more fluid than that and is actually a developing thing. We are constantly in the process of identifying others and identifying ourselves in relation to others (Brubaker and Cooper, 2000). So, if we identified ourselves as 'academics', what would we look like?

An answer based on stereotypes would see 'an academic' as the kind of person who thinks lofty thoughts and, having understood the learned articles and books which others have written, spends many months closeted away writing his/her own. This is, of course, a narrow, indeed archaic, view of academic identity which overly focuses on one aspect of the role. Boyer (1990) attempts to give a more rounded view of the work of academics; he suggests that academic work divides into four separate but overlapping functions, known as scholarships.

1. The scholarship of *discovery* approximates most closely to the stereotypical view of academic activity. Within this scholarship academics undertake their own original research and from this develop knowledge.

2. The scholarship of *application* suggests a less esoteric role for academics. Here they take what they know and apply it to solve practical, social problems. However, they do not simply apply discoveries from their own research in this way.

3. Instead, within the scholarship of *integration*, academics synthesise what they know across disciplines, people and time.

4. In the scholarship of *teaching*, later described as teaching and learning, Boyer suggests the study of teaching and learning practice also to be fundamental to the work of academics.

Case study

Figure 4.1 illustrates how these scholarships might interrelate in the work of Jo, a teacher educator who is preparing a presentation focusing on the development of pupil leadership in school.

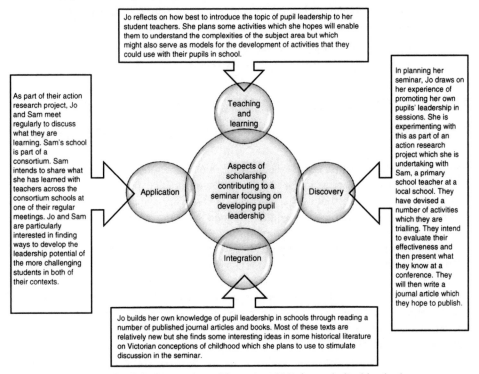

Figure 4.1 An example of the integration of Boyer's (1990) four scholarships in the preparatory work of a teacher educator for a seminar focusing on developing pupil leadership in school.

This example demonstrates how Jo uses the four scholarships together to support her own professional development and that of her colleague and student teachers. Jo draws on her experience of working with students to plan her session on pupil leadership. To supplement her learning from practice she also draws, through reading, on the practice and theory of others who are interested in this subject. Her ongoing research work allows her and her collaborator Sam to build knowledge which, through development and dissemination activity, has the potential to influence practice and understanding both locally and on a wider scale.

In adopting this integrated approach Jo is demonstrating what Hoyle (1975) refers to as extended professionality. According to Hoyle, restricted professionals value the day-to-day work of teaching, rely on intuition and sustain a classroom-based perspective. Extended professionals adopt an active approach to understanding professional needs and how to address them through enhanced communication with peers and engagement with theory. In other words, they engage with all aspects of the four scholarships to develop a full, balanced professional identity. I am suggesting that in the case of teacher educators such a balanced professional identity might properly be referred to as an academic identity.

Critical questions

» Which of the four scholarships is most central to your beliefs and actions as a teacher educator?

» What would be the challenges of developing those scholarships which are currently less influential in your professional life?

What benefit can the development of an academic identity bring to teacher educators?

You may already be enthusiastically embracing the challenge of developing all aspects of your academic identity as a teacher educator as defined by the four scholarships. Conversely, you may feel that such a challenge is irrelevant in your case. With limited time and energy available it can be argued that we need to make judgements about the relative worth of time spent on actually preparing for and leading a presentation, for example, as compared with time spent on background reading. The inevitable choice for many new teacher educators would be perhaps to focus on the teaching. Many studies, such as Hughes (2005), show that the correlation between the quality of teacher engagement with research and the quality of pupil learning is inconclusive. Others argue that the learning, thinking and professional stimulation associated with research activity can have a positive impact on the pupils we teach (Chetty and Lubben, 2010). This difference of view appears to derive from an understanding of the scholarships as separate entities which either happily exist alongside one another (Feather, 2010) or are in opposition to one another. Instead of viewing research and teaching as opposing elements which time and energy limitations force us to choose between, I would suggest that they are better viewed as complementary activities which, as demonstrated in Figure 4.1, can be mutually supportive in the complex process of facilitating student learning (Brew and Boud, 1995).

The potential enhancement of student learning arising from our full engagement with all four scholarships is one rationale for developing an academic identity and associated practices. However, both as teachers and teacher educators, our responsibility is not simply to teach individuals but to contribute to the wider development of knowledge in our field. Stenhouse's plea (1975) for teachers to research their own practice was driven by a belief that teachers are in a unique position to understand their world and thus improve it. Hargreaves (1996) and Goldacre (2013) similarly argued for the development of an evidenced-based teaching profession to underpin the improvement of practice. Wherever you are working as a teacher educator you are a part of our professional community. Knowledge creation and dissemination lie at the heart of this community and it is through the publication of the outcomes of research, by teachers and teacher educators amongst others, that such knowledge-building is achieved (Kamler, 2008).

Critical questions

» What are your views on the relationship between research and teaching in supporting the learning of student teachers?

» How do you respond to the suggestion that you have a responsibility to contribute to the wider development of knowledge in the field of teacher education?

How might an academic identity be developed?

If you have been convinced that the development of an academic aspect to your professional identity is a worthwhile endeavour, the question now becomes, how might you achieve that? You may find some of the following suggestions helpful.

Find something you are passionate about and focus your academic work on it

What are your professional values? What are your professional concerns? What excites you? What do you want to change? Focusing your research and writing on the areas which emerge from your answers to these questions will allow you to develop an academic identity which you really value (Lamont, 1992). Researching and writing about things you are passionate about, where you have a voice you wish to be heard and a position to uphold, is immensely satisfying (Savin-Baden, 2008). Conversely, consistently working to a research agenda that is not your own leads only to the development of an inauthentic self.

Start to read and write

The best way to develop your skills in writing about your research is just to start to write. It is a myth that most academics write easily, for, in fact, most of us find writing challenging. The only way to improve your writing is to keep writing. Reading can help with this. If you begin to read journal articles or books on the things you are passionate about, your reading will stimulate your thinking. You will either agree or disagree with what you have read. Your own opinions will be informed by the views of others. You can write about what you thought previously and what you now think, about what others think and how their thinking has influenced yours. In and through your writing you will firm up your views and find your own academic voice.

Find an academic community with similar values and interests to your own and become part of it

Becoming part of an academic community is another key facilitator of the development of an academic identity. Lave and Wenger (1991) refer to these as 'communities of practice'; that is, communities in which practices are shared and in which newcomers developing practice are supported by working alongside more experienced colleagues. It is often daunting to begin a research project on your own. It is even more daunting to write about it on your own. Working on early research and writing projects with a more experienced academic colleague is mutually beneficial and allows new teacher educators to find the confidence to continue to develop their academic practice and persona. It may appear more difficult for teacher educators within a school context to locate appropriate communities of practice. However, there are usually a number of opportunities to join in the activities of partners such as universities, other ITE providers or school alliances. In many areas groups of schools are also developing into communities which use scholarship activities to develop practice (see, for example, the story of the HertsCam Network at www.hertscam.org.uk). Working with others outside of your own institution can provide provocation to thinking and challenging of assumptions, which all academic endeavour requires. The example in Figure 4.1 of Jo and Sam's collaboration is based on such a cross-organisational partnership. Others include HEA groups, special interest groups within BERA, UCET and other bodies.

Share what you know with the wider academic community

A key lever in the development of an academic identity is sharing what you know. This is often challenging to new teacher educators who fear they may be made to feel inadequate or even ridiculed, whereas in reality the academic community is actually made up of people like you. As a starting point, attending and presenting at conferences on topics which are relevant to you will give you the opportunity to share your developing expertise with others who will be glad of the opportunity to learn from you. If conferences sound too daunting at this stage, you might consider writing a blog or an article for a professional journal while you develop confidence in your own voice.

IN A **NUTSHELL**

Developing an academic identity is not, then, about taking on a whole new persona. It is about continuing the process of identification, the evolving process of developing an identity, and integrating new ways of thinking, doing and being to strengthen your current values, beliefs and practices. Developing an academic identity means beginning to see yourself as an academic. This does not mean you have abandoned your commitment to students or to teaching and learning. On the contrary, it means that you have recommitted yourself to make use of all of the scholarships available to you, to ensure that you are preparing new or aspiring teachers for the complex demands now made of them as professional educators.

REFLECTIONS ON **CRITICAL ISSUES**

- *An academic identity can be explored through the framework of Boyer's four scholarships – (i) discovery, (ii) application, (iii) integration and (iv) teaching.*

- *The more you embrace an academic identity the more you will contribute to the learning of your students and the pupils in your school.*

- *Engaging with reading and writing and an academic community are the key tools in developing an academic identity. This is most effective when focused on your personal professional interests.*

Part B

Institutional models

CHAPTER 5

WHAT DOES OUTSTANDING SCHOOL-BASED TEACHER EDUCATION LOOK LIKE?

Liz White and Kim Jones

CRITICAL **ISSUES**

- *How do we define 'outstanding'?*
- *To what outcomes do we aspire?*
- *What kinds of partnership have the synergy to bring about outstanding provision?*
- *How will we know what the impact of our provision has been?*

What do we mean by outstanding practice in student teachers?

Outstanding school-based teacher education may be viewed as the provision of ITE that develops the capability of student teachers to become expert teachers in their future career. We use the term 'student teachers with outstanding practice' rather than 'outstanding teachers', since by the time student teachers qualify, they are likely to have had the opportunity to demonstrate outstanding practice only in a limited range of contexts, with limited groups of pupils in a particular subject area. The term 'outstanding' can bring negative inferences of compliance and prescription. School inspectors look for outstanding teaching that matches defined criteria, and student teachers (along with all other qualified teachers) are assessed against standards, for example the Teachers' Standards (DfE, 2012b) in England. In these descriptions 'outstanding' teaching is based on what is currently considered to raise attainment of pupils. This assumes that effective teaching will result in learning taking place for all pupils and that this will be reflected in pupil attainment in tests. Education can have many aims, of which raising attainment is only one, albeit an important one, especially for governments and those funding educational establishments. Pupil achievement is intrinsically linked with issues of social class, peer influence and the social capital of their community. Therefore, rather than narrowly describing 'outstanding practice' as facilitating pupils to achieve high levels of attainment in assessments, we would like to offer some provocations to help to expand the vision for teacher education.

The question is 'What does outstanding practice look like?' rather than 'What does outstanding practice produce?' We do not want to provide a tick-box set of criteria here but to promote a set of values and attitudes that underpin our practice and uphold our sense of moral purpose. Definitions of what we mean by outstanding practice are socially constructed and influenced by our culture (Troman, 1996; Berliner, 2001). What is seen as outstanding in one context may not be in another, and where cultural changes are rapid and success measures change, there may also be a rapid change in what is seen as the best pedagogy and practice in teaching. For example, in secondary science teaching in England there was a change in focus from skills to knowledge in the space of a decade. In 2000 there was great emphasis on learning by discovery and through experimentation, and a pupil's ability to hypothesise, plan and successfully carry out their own experiment safely was the key to gaining a large proportion of the marks in exams. By 2010 the emphasis had shifted entirely to being able to analyse and draw conclusions from given results, being able to use standard scientific terms accurately and being able to apply knowledge to new theoretical situations. Very little practical experimentation remained in the course and none at all in the exam.

The development of expertise as a teacher has been characterised by five stages on a continuum (Alexander, 2010) from novice, through advanced beginner, competent and proficient to expert. Here, expertise is described in relation to how professional knowledge is used intuitively due to experience. The complexity of personal and professional development makes it unlikely that such linear progression is the reality for many teachers, and additionally, as Eaude (2012) points out, the level of expertise of any teacher will differ according to the subject they are teaching, the context and pupils' background, age and culture.

Outstanding teaching occurs when interventions are planned in response to how pupils are learning and the style of pedagogy is appropriate for the learning intentions, the pupils and the subject matter. This requires the teacher to have considerable interpersonal skills, creativity and a passion for learning and teaching and for the subject content. With the current drive for developing independent learners there is a need to cultivate a deep understanding in pupils to enable them to be charting their own way through their learning and determining their own learning outcomes. The personal development of pupils is an important aspect of their learning, and requires a more holistic approach than drilling in subject knowledge and examination techniques.

The learning teacher is a useful concept here, as an ongoing professional stance, with the teacher being a lifelong learner and modelling learning for their pupils. Learning teachers are open to new ideas and involved in the construction and reconstruction of professional knowledge through reflecting on practice. In this way the teacher shares in the learning experience with the pupils, making sense of the subject knowledge together, confident to allow learners to question, explore and discover for themselves and sharing in the excitement of their new findings. Linking with this concept, student teachers and experienced teachers can helpfully be viewed as *learning teaching* rather than embarking on a programme *to learn to teach* (Lampert, 2010). 'Learning teaching' suggests that learning occurs while doing the work both during ITE and when qualified rather than the practice of teaching occurring in the future, after a distinct portion of knowledge is learned. Bell and Cordingley (2014) found that in exceptional schools involved in ITE, teachers were more aware of the professional learning of their leaders, which reflects this development of a learning community, where learning is valued by all.

Critical questions

» What do you mean by 'outstanding practice' as a teacher?

» How is professional learning valued in your setting throughout a teacher's career?

What does outstanding provision of teacher education look like?

The aspiration of outstanding providers of ITE is to afford all student teachers the opportunity, challenge and support that they need to reach their full potential through their teacher education, to become outstanding teachers and school leaders. All partners in the provision strive together to build the programme by listening to the stakeholders and being responsive to their changing needs, and being committed to undertaking further improvements and developments which promote the following principles:

» to recognise the individuality of student teachers: their pre-training experience, knowledge and skills, and their ITE needs;

» to educate student teachers to be the best teachers they can be, to enable them to embark confidently on their NQT year and beyond;

» to ensure student teachers have a clear understanding of learning theories and child development and how this impacts on pupil learning and informs their own development as a teacher;

» to be able to critically analyse, engage in and reflect on educational issues, philosophies and initiatives;

» to maintain as central the entitlement of school children to receive a high-quality education.

Working with these principles, different themes emerge in the examples of provision explored in the following chapters. One of these themes is developing an ethos where all partners in the provision *share high aspirations*. This goes beyond ensuring consistency of judgements through quality assurance (QA) across the programme and is explored in Chapters 7 and 8. In Chapter 7 the importance of all partners recognising that they have equal responsibility and accountability for success within a small partnership, as well as the necessity of recognising and valuing the contribution all partners make being crucial to continuing success, is considered. Van Velzen and Timmermans (Chapter 8) describe exploratory attempts to maximise learning in school context through the use of the collaborative mentoring approach rather than reproducing the teaching approaches used in the HEI context.

Where schools are advancing in their leadership of ITE, the need to provide an expansive learning environment for teachers which offers a breadth of learning opportunities and a culture that promotes learning, should be recognised. Hodgkinson and Hodgkinson (2005) described a continuum of expansive-restrictive learning environments for teachers, where the expansive learning environment provided:

» close collaborative working;

» mutually supportive colleagues;

» an explicit focus on teacher learning and supportive opportunities for personal development beyond institutional priorities;

» time to reflect;

» a wide range of learning opportunities.

Research from exceptional schools involved in ITE similarly indicates that there is a consistent focus on collaborative working, extensive community networks and partnerships with local organisations. Teachers within these schools are enthusiastically leading their own professional learning (Bell and Cordingley, 2014). Teachers, including mentors and school leaders, will make a significant contribution in creating an expansive learning environment in their context.

Another theme is that of *developing the ability of student teachers to reflect* on their reading, observations and experiences. Reflective practice is much more than just thinking about teaching, but involves a constant critical look at teaching and learning in order to improve practice. Schön (2003) suggests that reflection-in-action is the almost unconscious, immediate reflection that happens as a more experienced teacher deals with issues in the classroom, and reflection-on-action takes place after the event and is more deliberate. This is the process that can involve mentors and tutors in lesson observation feedback and supporting student teachers in the accuracy and objectivity of their self-evaluation. In the latter process, intuitive professional knowing can be made explicit, and teacher educators will need to be able to articulate this with their student teachers (Chapter 3, Field). Developing reflective practitioners is one of the most challenging roles for teacher educators because of the nebulous nature of the skills involved. This requires mentors who are both highly reflective themselves and understand fully how to develop this skill in their student teachers (Chapter 7, Jones). Reflective practice is a strong strategy for bridging the theory-practice divide.

Teacher education is profoundly important and complicated, but poorly understood. To create effective teachers who have a positive impact on the learning and personal development of their pupils, we need high-quality teacher education led by teacher educators who, in turn, have their professional development needs met. This is not least because the learning of student teachers is directly affected by who is teaching them as much as by the content of the programme (Furlong et al, 2000). Part A provided some useful prompts regarding identity, knowledge and skills for the individual professional development of teacher educators. These aspects are explored further in the handbook *School-Based Teacher Training* (White and Jarvis, 2013).

Critical questions

» What do you (as a provider) and your partners mean by 'outstanding practice' in teacher education?

» What contribution do you make in providing an expansive learning environment for student teachers and for those involved in teacher education in your setting?

» How are you nurturing your teacher educators?

Ways in which collaborative partnerships bring about outstanding provision

In the current landscape schools have the opportunity to be involved in ITE in a variety of ways. The phrase 'school-led' ITE refers to the role of the school within the provision, whereas 'school-centred' and 'school-based' ITE refers to the location of the student teachers at given points in the programme. In England some school-led provision is in collaborative partnership with HEIs while some Teaching School Alliances are building their own provision independently. This current drive towards school-led provision requires schools to take more responsibility for the nature of teacher education and development of the profession. While welcomed by some, this transition presents a major challenge for all partners in setting up and maintaining quality ITE provision.

Both Roberts (Chapter 4) and Jones (Chapter 7) consider ways of *building a learning community* focusing on the learning of both pupils, student teachers and the rest of the school community, and beyond, through different networks. These collaborative partnerships often develop into communities using scholarship and research activities to develop practice. Jones also shares how professional mentors working synergistically across the partnership can enhance the provision by ensuring the best practice from each partnership school contributes to the collaborative whole. Individual schools can benefit greatly from their involvement in constructing this growing body of knowledge to which they now have access. Although it continually takes a lot of hard work to develop and maintain a strong partnership with good communication links, the rewards and benefits of being involved in such partnerships are immeasurable. Creating a new partnership for the provision of ITE is not about merely imitating good practice found in other providers, as each partnership should have its own unique identity arising from the diversity within the group of schools and the accrediting body.

Chapman (Chapter 6) and van Velzen and Timmermans (Chapter 7) have all been developing collaborative practice in school-based ITE through *inquiry-based approaches*. An appreciative inquiry into a new approach across partnership schools working with an HEI has been used to enhance the quality of provision and strengthen the sense of partnership (Chapter 6, Chapman). Sometimes the learning opportunities available in school are not fully exploited for the benefit of student teachers. The collaborative mentoring approach described in Chapter 8 (van Velzen and Timmermans) provides a tool for SBTEs to use to model and scaffold the learning in such a way that learning opportunities are maximised.

Beyond the internal partnerships that ITE providers establish, there is also an important role for an external, critical friend to develop the provision further, whether through the position of external examiner for an HEI or as an external moderator for school-centred provision. The choice of critical friend needs to be influenced by geographical location (to avoid direct competitors) as well as by a common vision.

Critical questions

» Who are your collaborative partners in ITE?

» Are you getting the best from collaboration?

» Can you define what makes your provision unique?

Researching and evaluating the impact of our provision

From the outset it is important to have an overview of how the partnership is developing. Agreement needs to be reached within the partnership as to how the *impact of the ITE* will be measured, and this should be formalised. When new strategies are employed the effectiveness of these must be evaluated and decisions made about the way forward. This is illustrated by the research carried out by Chapman (Chapter 6) and van Velzen and Timmermans (Chapter 8).

Intelligent use of data to monitor the impact of ITE and identify areas for development and improvement is discussed by Jones (Chapter 7). In order to collect reliable data it is important to use both soft and hard data from all stakeholders. This allows you to triangulate your data and ensure that you are not responding to views held by only a small number of participants. Even after data have been collected and trends are identified they need to be used intelligently to navigate your future path.

Critical questions

» How are you measuring the impact of your provision?

» Are you getting the outcomes to which you aspire?

IN A **NUTSHELL**

Outstanding teaching can be narrowly viewed as involving carefully planned lessons that meet specified objectives. In this chapter a broader understanding is proposed, where teaching is responsive and interactive, drawing on a high level of professional knowing, skills and passion, both with respect to subject area and the group of learners.

Outstanding teacher education affords student teachers expansive learning environments to learn alongside more experienced teachers; high aspirations are shared across the partnership and opportunities to reflect are facilitated. Meeting the professional development needs of teacher educators will be vital to ensuring the continued quality of the provision. To assure the ongoing quality, systems need to be in place that give regular feedback from all stakeholders.

REFLECTIONS ON **CRITICAL ISSUES**

- *In using the term 'outstanding' we have to be clear what we are aiming for in our practice as teacher educators.*

- *It is just as crucial to provide excellent professional development for your teacher educators as for your student teachers.*

- *Thoughtful use of data ensures continuing high-quality ITE.*

CHAPTER 6 | WHAT PEDAGOGICAL APPROACH IS NEEDED IN SCHOOL-LED TRAINING TO DEVELOP OUTSTANDING TEACHERS?

Lynn Chapman

CRITICAL **ISSUES**

- *How can HEIs and schools work effectively together in partnership?*
- *How can the appreciative inquiry model of change theory help to form a strong partnership?*
- *How can HEI/school partnerships address the theory/practice divide?*
- *What is an appropriate structure and content for school-led ITE?*

Recent government-led changes to teacher education in England have resulted in the requirement to increase school-led ITE using expert practitioners to complement the work of teacher educators based in universities. Building on the excellent partnership already in existence between our university and local schools, we set out to jointly develop a set of school-led units of work to draw on the expertise of both teachers in school and IBTEs. The aim of each unit was to allow student teachers to focus on learning and teaching and create the opportunity for observation, reflection and consideration of theory, to enable them to identify good practice that could be applied to their own teaching.

Change is a daunting prospect for most people, and recent changes in ITE require HEIs and schools to work together in new ways – and this is a challenge. A major barrier to effecting change is when people feel uninvolved in the change process, often experiencing change as something that is 'done to them' with the inevitable feelings of lack of control and low morale that follows. Change can also bring to the surface a number of negative feelings, especially if the starting premise is to look at the issue in terms of 'what isn't working' and 'how to fix the problem' (Seel, 2008). An alternative to this deficit model of change management is a solution-focused approach, to look at what is working well already and using that as a starting point. Appreciative inquiry, founded by David Cooperrider, is one such solution-focused approach (Cooperrider and Whitney, 2005). The key to understanding this as a process of change is in the very words themselves used to describe the process – *appreciative* identifies and celebrates what is already working well and *inquiry* is a way to explore new possibilities building on existing success (McDrury and Alterio, 2003). Appreciative inquiry therefore begins with the stories of success, draws out the good and the positive and ignores stories of failure. While this may seem unrealistic in a world of 'problems and failures', there is good evidence to suggest that a focus on positive reinforcement can have constructive and long-lasting effects.

There are five stages in the process of appreciative inquiry (Lewis et al, 2011); each of these steps and how they were used to both define and effect a change in school-led ITE has been briefly outlined below.

Step 1 – Define

The first step is to be very clear from the outset about the purpose of change, in order to establish clear outcomes. Our aim was to find a sustainable way to facilitate school-led teacher education by working in partnership with a number of secondary schools to design and deliver outstanding ITE. It would be tempting (and more usual) to start by focusing on all the problems and deficiencies of implementing such a programme. As an alternative, we identified and reinforced the partnership's strengths, achievements and vision by focusing on what was already working well. Framing this as an inquiry question – 'In what ways can we develop school-led ITE to improve the programme and enhance outcomes for our student teachers?' – helped us to keep focused on the positive aspects.

Step 2 – Discovery: identifying the best of what already works

This phase is about pulling out underlying positive themes to identify the strengths and core values of the group, and a central feature in order to achieve this is talking about stories of success. A key principle of appreciative inquiry is that only when people share stories of good practice and moments when they have felt highly effective do they begin to feel both empowered and that they have a key part to play in effecting change. By making explicit and sharing what is often tacit knowledge, effective and good working practices that are already in place can be highlighted. It is also an act of self-review and helps us make sense of, and make connections between, thought and feeling. Members of the group themselves are therefore at the heart of creating the vision for change, and because of their central role during this phase their vision has more likelihood of becoming reality. Through the telling of our stories of success we identified three key themes that became threaded through, and embedded in, the subsequent stages of the process:

- » the power of true *collaboration*;
- » the *creation of something new*;
- » *dedication* to making the student teacher experience better.

To act as a stimulus to eliciting stories, we used the following key questions:

- » What does the university already do well?
- » What do schools already do well?
- » What do we already do well in partnership?

We found stories more informative than generalised answers to these questions due to the fact that they are situated in a particular context and have the added power and impact of evoking emotion.

Step 3 – Dream: what might be? – envisioning the results

This phase has two stages: to create the visions that address the structure and functions of the group, following on from the capacity-building exercise of the Discovery phase; and to create the visions that articulate the long-term aims.

A powerful question that is useful to ask at this stage is 'What would things be like if...?' as it encourages reflective thinking and provides the space for more creative ideas to flow. The Dream phase is the lynchpin of the whole appreciative inquiry cycle as it acts as a bridge between the best of *what already is* and the group's speculation of *what might be*. This can be summed up in a propositional statement (see below) which is used to guide the planning and future working of the group. Note how it is written in both a positive tone and in the present tense.

Our university and school partnership is a learning organisation that fosters the sharing of ideas and harnesses the synergy of group cooperation to create new ideas and new ways of working that go beyond what any one individual can produce alone. Our partnership accelerates its learning through regular (termly) meetings that involve all members of the partnership. As a setting for 'strategic learning', members present their success stories to help create the environment for reflection and share new innovations to provide a model of excellent teacher education.

To complete the propositional statement we also incorporated the attributes we wanted to create in our student teachers in order to define the result of our outstanding ITE as follows:

Our student teachers:

- *know how children learn appropriate to their age and stage of learning and are able to draw on learning theories and the latest research to come to informed opinions;*
- *have the ability to research in depth and apply acquired knowledge to their own practice;*
- *have the flexibility to adapt to, and learn from, different contexts;*
- *are resilient, on both a professional and personal level, and are able to cope with uncertainty;*
- *have the ability to reflect and take appropriate action;*
- *are innovative, imaginative and discerning risk takers;*
- *demonstrate professionalism at all times;*
- *are highly employable.*

A good propositional statement will stretch and challenge the group and drive it to achieve more, be grounded in possibility and be highly participative, requiring effort from all members of the group.

Step 4 – Design

With the creation of the dream now complete, the Design phase is to develop strategies to achieve that dream. The outcome of this phase is a set of practical steps that define and direct the actions of both the group and individuals. For us it was helpful to create the following action plan:

What: produce the outline of six discrete units of work with clearly defined outcomes for student teachers;

Why: support professional mentors in facilitating learning in school and ensure equity of opportunity and consistency of outcomes for student teachers across all participating schools;

How: create units of work around six themes: Structuring Learning; Behaviour for Learning; Collaborative Learning; Assessment for Learning; Inclusion and Questioning;

Who: teams of university tutors and professional mentors.

It was important during this phase to keep in mind our goal of creating an innovative approach to school-led ITE. In order to achieve that goal we needed to go beyond current approaches.

Step 5 – Delivery

This stage is characterised by implementing the action plan, which required a great deal of preparation by all members of the group. Having identified the themes it was agreed that one theme would be the focus of each of six days divided equally between the autumn and spring terms. We focused on finding a common structure for each day and divided into smaller groups to plan and produce resources. Prior to the first school-led session, the whole group met to talk through the programme for each day and to provide support, particularly for those less experienced as teacher educators. After the first three days, the leaders reviewed the sessions giving feedback on what had gone well and sharing improvements and adaptations, in order to inform the teaching of the final three units. Feedback was very positive with professional mentors reporting:

» good quality resources meant they were clear about their role;

» how well the structure of each day supported the learning outcomes;

» a previously unforeseen benefit – the willingness of teachers to become involved and who were now actively asking to have student teachers observe them teach in order to share their expertise and good practice.

This has led to a renewed focus on learning and teaching as a whole-school initiative in these schools.

Critical questions

» How could you use appreciative inquiry for developing your partnership provision?

» Are there more creative approaches that could come from the strengths of your partnership?

The gap between theory and practice has been well documented (Korthagen et al, 2001) and it is now widely accepted that simply transmitting theoretical knowledge about teaching in the hope that student teachers will apply this in the classroom is not effective. While there has been a move towards more school-based teacher education in recent years, without consideration of the pedagogy of ITE there is no guarantee that the extra time in school alone will bridge the theory/practice divide (Chapter 3, Field). Since good teaching cannot simply be mimicked, observation of practising teachers without a clear focus and without guided reflection by experts is unlikely to lead to better outcomes in practice. It was with this in mind that we used the move towards more school-based (i.e. located in a school) and school-led (i.e. taught by a practising teacher) sessions as an opportunity to do something different. At the heart of what we wanted to create was a seamless transition between the theory of teaching and its practice and to showcase excellent teaching. This would give student teachers the opportunity to reflect and to consider the impact on their own teaching. This works in practice by a senior member of the teaching staff leading a group of 10 to 15 student teachers. Each day begins with a one-hour workshop to introduce and highlight the theme, which is then analysed to allow student teachers to begin to consider what good practice looks like and make the all-important links to the underlying pedagogy. In the *Structuring Learning* unit, student teachers:

» are introduced to the language of objectives and outcomes;

» consider 'Why do we need objectives and outcomes?';

» consider 'What makes a successful lesson?';

» are shown supporting video clips highlighting good practice.

In order for student teachers to see the pedagogy working in practice, this workshop is immediately followed by a focused observation of one or two lessons guided by an observation sheet, which directs them to look for the very points that have been highlighted in the previous session. Student teachers are divided into small groups for these observations, to allow them to compare notes and discuss their observations and reflect on what they have seen in order to identify best practice. Essential to the success of these observations is to brief the observed teachers, so they are aware of what student teachers are looking for and are therefore able to ensure they demonstrate and make explicit their good practice. Finally the senior teacher facilitates a session of guided reflection to encourage student teachers to consider what they have observed and how it links to the underlying pedagogy. Student teachers use a reflective log to record what they have learnt. They then consider how this will impact on their own practice and identify strategies they will develop to trial in their own lessons.

Student teachers consistently report that they appreciate their school-led days and that the structure helps them to immediately see how the theory is put into practice. Independently commissioned research confirms this and our own exit data confirms good progress and outcomes of student teachers.

The research sought to find out to what extent the links between theory and practice are strengthened, the kind of reflection student teachers are able to engage in and how they are able to apply the good practice they identify. Below are some of the comments of student teachers.

Referring to seeing the theory in practice they told us:

I had a very positive experience of the lead school, it was very well organised. The staff took it very seriously and placed us in lessons where the teachers were very aware of what we were learning about and they actively showed us examples of it ... we then did interviews with pupils to find out how they had found the techniques used ... things I thought I could learn from, I incorporated into my teaching.

We could have just been at university and learned but the good thing was that immediately after we discussed an idea we could go and watch it in practice and know specifically what we were looking at and what we were looking for.

They showed that they were able to reflect on their own practice. One said:

There was an instance with Year 11. They didn't do anything at first – had no interest in anything to do with subject. Actually I got to know them, to find what makes them tick and I realised they weren't trying because they thought they were going to fail ... so I had to work out ways in which they could feel they were succeeding. It's all about problem-solving and I like that about teaching.

Student teachers were able to give examples of how to put good practice into their own teaching:

Before I tried to put questions in my lessons but they may not have been very good ones, but I hadn't really thought about it like that before [the day on questioning] so if they were good it was more out of luck than knowing why they were good. So after that day I started putting questions into my planning and then having them written for the beginning and end of lessons. That definitely helped me to get better.

Critical question

» Are you certain that your student teachers are making the vital links between theory and practice?

IN A **NUTSHELL**

The move towards a more school-led/school-based approach to ITE should be seen as an opportunity to improve current practice. It is perhaps part of our culture to look for reasons why something cannot or will not work, which may, in part, be due to the more traditional deficit models we are used to employing when effecting change. Appreciative inquiry offers a more positive approach, and it certainly enabled us to work together in true partnership to create something that was better than either party could have achieved alone. It also enabled us to address the issue of the theory-practice divide and start to bridge that gap. Having learnt a great deal from this experience, we have embarked on a further cycle of appreciative inquiry to look at building on our stories of success and expanding our model of school-led and school-based teacher education within the partnership.

REFLECTIONS ON **CRITICAL ISSUES**

- *The appreciative inquiry model provides a useful structure to facilitate strong partnership working because of the positive solution focus to this model.*
- *The role of the HEI in the partnership was to provide the provocation to move practice forward, the oversight to ensure consistency and to give SBTEs confidence in their role leading school-based sessions.*
- *The school-led and school-based aspects of the pedagogical approach described enabled student teachers to make clear links between theory and practice.*

Kim Jones

CRITICAL **ISSUES**

- *How do you maintain an ethos of high aspiration?*
- *How is an effective learning community built?*
- *How are student teachers developed as reflective practitioners?*
- *How is the impact of teacher education evaluated?*

Introduction

Alban Federation was established nine years ago by a group of secondary schools in Hertfordshire, England, all of which were experiencing difficulties in recruitment, particularly in shortage subjects. A rich vein of local residents who had the qualifications, aspirations and potential to make high-quality recruits to the teaching profession was identified, so the collective decision was made to become directly involved in ITE provision and to 'grow our own teachers'.

All the schools had excellent local reputations, and this set the tenor of high expectations that is a strong characteristic of the partnership. It was vital that the partnership could train teachers who were highly competent and professional by the end of their ITE and who demonstrated the potential to progress rapidly in the profession to positions of responsibility once they had completed their NQT year. QTS (Qualified Teacher Status) was awarded, meaning that this route into teaching was less academic than a PGCE but focused on developing the 'craft and professional persona' of the teacher.

Setting an ethos of high aspiration

Although developed from a group of high-performing schools it was not assumed that high expectations would automatically be part of the ITE partnership. It was important to develop our own culture and ethos that was linked to the identity of the partnership and not the schools. In early discussions it was agreed that we would embrace the following:

» a culture of high aspiration that would be shared and be evident across all stakeholders;

» all student teachers would be supported to develop the skills, values and attitudes to equip them for success in the classroom, the profession and the rapidly changing world of education;

» the taught course would meet the personal and professional needs of developing teachers and empower them as both learners and teachers;

» learning for all student teachers would be experiential and personalised.

This presented two challenges. The first was to ensure that the ethos was evident regardless of which partnership school you were in. The second was that this had to be applied to a diverse group of students with often widely varying needs including different:

» prior experience – ranging from those with none to those with experience as unqualified teachers;

» skills and talents;

» confidence and motivation levels;

» learning styles;

» personal circumstances.

It has long been recognised that the culture of an organisation is influenced by its leaders (Bass and Avolio, 1993) so it was vital that the heads of the schools were fully supportive of the partnership, frequently spoke of it in staff meetings and other forums and reinforced its ethos within their own school. Accountability for the success of the partnership is also held by the heads who, together with the partnership co-ordinator, comprise the management board. Termly board meetings that focus on strategic planning are attended by all the heads and annual reviews are conducted of their school and its contribution to the partnership. This overt support is a crucial factor in developing and sustaining the identity of the partnership.

High-quality support for new mentors is essential to maintain high aspirations. An audit is made of the skills and experience of every new mentor, and personalised professional development is planned. Most commonly this involves 'buddying' with an experienced mentor whom they shadow initially and who coach them as they develop their skills. The consistency of mentoring across the partnership is monitored through cross-moderation carried out by the professional mentors who are responsible for quality assuring the provision.

From the outset there were high expectations of student teachers. The partnership has a rigorous four-stage selection process which ensures that those accepted for the programme are of high calibre and have clear potential to become outstanding teachers. These stages are:

» initial check that applicants meet the statutory and partnership requirements;

» initial visit to a partnership school to give both the school and the applicant the opportunity to decide if this would be suitable for them;

» interview of applicants on school selection day by the head, subject specialists and a pupil panel when they may be asked to teach a lesson;

» formal interview by a professional panel.

Student teachers are supported throughout the programme by committed and experienced subject and professional mentors who devote their time and energy to providing support, modelling excellent practice and delivering high-quality teacher education. Consistency across the partnership is ensured by frequent communication between all those involved. All of the schools involved have a strong ethos of professional development, drawing on the experience and expertise within their school and other local schools. Teachers in the partnership schools are quick to recognise the opportunities of being involved in a successful ITE programme and develop professionally by acting as mentors.

Critical questions

» In what ways do you ensure that an ethos of high aspiration is maintained across your provision?

» How are new teacher educators inducted into your programme?

Building an effective learning community

Eight characteristics of effective learning communities have been identified. We wanted to build these into our partnership:

1. *shared values and vision;*
2. *collective responsibility for pupils' learning;*
3. *collaboration focused on learning;*
4. *individual and collective professional learning;*
5. *reflective professional enquiry;*
6. *openness, networks and partnerships;*
7. *inclusive membership;*
8. *mutual trust, respect and support.*

(Bolam et al, 2005, p i)

We believed a key strength of the new partnership was that the programme would be entirely school-based, in a context where professional learning was already embedded into an existing community of practice. SBTEs delivered the taught course, and there was a large degree of experiential learning (Lave and Wenger, 1991). It was crucial for all of the schools in the partnership to have an equal stake in, and equal responsibility for, the provision. Research and discussion culminated in a shared vision of teacher education, agreement about the experiential aspect of the programme and a shared and rigorous QA process. While acknowledging that the programme would have a less academic focus it was still seen as essential for it to have academic rigour and for the student teachers to recognise and immerse themselves in their role as learners. All of the partners were involved in devising a professional studies course which addressed this. This course, which addressed all aspects of educational theory and practice, drew on the skill and expertise of SBTEs and those already involved in the professional learning of teachers, resulting in high-quality teacher education.

From the outset, the vital nature of the student teacher/mentor relationship was recognised. Those who acted as subject mentors for student teachers were required to:

> » take on the role of critical friend;
> » have expert subject knowledge;
> » be able to model outstanding teaching;
> » have the skills to observe teaching and give constructive and developmental feedback.

The critical friend aspect was central to the relationship. The mentor needs to foster a relationship based on trust and support while still providing challenge. As defined by Costa and Kallick, a critical friend will:

> • *be clear about the nature of the relationship, and not use it for evaluation or judgment;*
> • *listen well: clarifying ideas, encouraging specificity, and taking time to fully understand what is being presented;*
> • *offer value judgments only upon request from the learner;*
> • *respond to the learner's work with integrity; and*
> • *be an advocate for the success of the work.*

(Costa and Kallick, 1993, p 50)

The partnership has an extensive group of experienced subject mentors, many of whom have taken several student teachers 'under their wing' over the years. A number of current subject mentors are former student teachers employed in partnership schools. They relish the opportunity to offer to others the same high-quality mentoring that they experienced.

The fact that the student teacher spends the entirety of their programme in a school experiencing all aspects of the teacher's professional role is seen as a key strength because, in addition to acquiring their classroom-based skills, they participate in all aspects of school life, for example pastoral responsibilities, undertaking statutory duties, teaching of life skills, participating in parent consultation evenings, writing reports and offering extra-curricular activities. In our experience, the outcome of this immersion in the role is teachers who are extremely well prepared for their NQT year.

A further strength of the partnership is the commitment and expertise of the professional mentors, one from each school, all of whom are highly experienced teachers and teacher educators. This group meet on a monthly basis and this frequency of contact is the 'glue' that holds the partnership together. At these monthly meetings the progress of each student teacher is reviewed, QA information is evaluated and this information is used to inform both operational and strategic planning. They are responsible for the smooth running of the partnership within their schools, including the professional studies course. The programme draws on the strengths of staff across all schools in the partnership and enables student teachers to gain experience in each of the schools.

The high success rates and high retention rates and evidence that former student teachers move rapidly into positions of responsibility are all strong indicators that all of these factors work together very efficiently and the outcome is a highly effective learning community.

Critical questions

» In what ways are you building a learning community across your provision?

» Who are your key people and how do you provide professional learning opportunities for them to develop further?

Developing student teachers as reflective practitioners

One development in teacher education over the past decade has been the focus on the importance of teachers being skilled reflective practitioners:

Teacher educators who represent a variety of conceptual and ideological orientations to schooling and teacher education have, under the umbrella of reflective practice, tried to prepare teachers who are more thoughtful and analytic about their work.

(Zeichner, 2005c, p 9)

Developing student teachers as reflective practitioners is often the aspect which is a challenge to teacher educators because of the abstract nature of the skills involved. One of the hurdles is to move the student teacher from vague generalisations to making focused observations supported by evidence. The focus is on the individual development of student teachers' practical skills and the need to ensure the pupils they teach make at least good progress in their learning. A key skill of an outstanding teacher is high-quality reflection on learning and teaching, both their own and their pupils'. This requires a mentor who can both model reflective practice and ask questions that elicit reflective responses.

The relationship between subject mentors and student teachers is central to this and, in our partnership, is developed prior to the programme when they work together on an introductory day to carry out an initial needs analysis. This allows time for an extended dialogue where the student teacher is encouraged to reflect on their prior experience against the Teachers' Standards (DfE, 2012b) and to begin to identify their own learning needs with guidance from the subject mentor.

Student teachers meet weekly with their subject mentors for a formal meeting. The importance of this is recognised by making it a condition of the partnership agreement to which all schools have signed up. The main purpose is to develop the skill of reflective practice. The subject mentor will lead and guide the student teacher to reflect on their progress in their teaching against the Teachers' Standards (DfE, 2012b). They do this by asking questions and giving feedback on, for example, observed lessons or seminar papers, where they might model the language of the profession and reflective practice. The balance in these meetings subtly changes through the year as the student teacher develops their skill of reflection and the role of the subject mentor changes from that of modeller and guide to that of challenger and critical friend. By the end, student teachers should be able to apply this skill to all aspects of their professional development and continue to do so throughout their career.

There is some debate as to the extent of reflective practice that should be employed. Some believe that its use should be applied only to learning that takes place in the classroom, that is lesson evaluation. This view is reflected in the Teachers' Standards (DfE, 2012b) which require teachers to '*reflect systematically on the effectiveness of lessons and approaches to teaching*'. Others believe that it is a vital tool for teachers to apply to all aspects of their professional life and should equally be used to identify their own learning needs throughout their careers (Day and Harris, 2002).

Our partnership takes the latter view, and throughout the year student teachers are required to keep a reflective journal written on a weekly basis. This has a different purpose to the formal reflective practice and is more personal to the student teacher, encouraging them to focus on their feelings rather than analysing situations. It is often an enlightening read and student teachers describe it as cathartic.

Evaluating the impact of teacher education

Whoever came up with the adage that 'weighing the pig won't make it fatter' understood the importance of intelligent use of data. Strong QA mechanisms are central to the evaluation process. You can analyse and triangulate the data but unless you use it to inform strategic planning you are still just 'weighing the pig'.

One of the easiest ways to get a feel for impact is to look at outcomes, how many student teachers are:

» successfully completing the programme;

» being graded good or outstanding on completion;

» still in teaching three years after completion.

This is one measure of success but it does not give any information about why you have achieved this. Gaining an accurate overview involves collecting a wide range of soft and hard data from all stakeholders. Soft data includes views and opinions while hard data is that to which a numerical value can be attached and which can be statistically analysed. It is important to collect hard data on a continuing basis, especially if you are a small provider with relatively few student teachers in each cohort as the following example illustrates.

Case study

A small provider collecting data on student teachers being graded outstanding on completion collects the following data over six years:

YEAR	Number	%
2007	6 of 10	60%
2008	4 of 12	33%
2009	8 of 14	57.1%
2010	5 of 13	38.5%
2011	9 of 12	75%
2012	5 of 11	45.5%

Taken as individual sets of data this gives widely fluctuating information. In the 75% year they would be very pleased with their data but some of the intervening years suggest a very different story. If, however, the running data is calculated, then their average rate for students achieving outstanding is 51.675% which gives a more reliable overview of this aspect but still tells nothing about the reasons for it.

Comparison of hard data is one of the ways in which the success of providers is measured by the government. Far more important in the example above would be to determine whether the fluctuation was purely due to small numbers in each cohort or whether there are issues to be addressed. For example, was there an element to the course in 2011 that supported such strong outcomes that was not replicated in 2012.

Collecting the views of stakeholders gives invaluable feedback in circumstances such as this but this needs to be done systematically through tools such as standardised questionnaires. We collected a wide range of soft data including views from the following:

» potential student teachers (regarding the interview and selection process);

» student teachers;

» ex-student teachers (NQTs);

» subject mentors;

» professional mentors;

» head teachers.

It is relatively easy to convert this type of soft data into hard data by asking those being surveyed to grade each statement on the questionnaire. There is also information to be gleaned from comments, so a questionnaire that combines both gives the optimum amount of information. While it is tempting to 'tweak' questionnaires each year there needs to be a core of standard questions so that you can measure progress.

If the data you collect is rich and well triangulated (common views expressed by all stakeholders), it should give a clear overview of strengths and areas for development. The hard data for the latter should transfer into your improvement plan as baseline data against which progress can be measured. The next step is strategic planning of the action that needs to be taken to secure change or improvement. Here soft data is also vital as the feedback from stakeholders helps clarify where issues lie and may contain valuable suggestions that you can utilise. This planning is then converted into targets in your improvement plan. The continued collection of hard data gives evidence for measuring progress from the baseline and enables you to make clear judgements about the impact of your actions. The soft data will continue to give information about responses to the strategies. This works equally well for short timescale changes as well as for more long-term projects.

IN A **NUTSHELL**

From the outset you must have clear vision about what steps you need to take to build an effective learning community and how you will first achieve and then maintain an ethos of high aspiration across your partnership. It is just as important to develop your teacher educators as your student teachers. You need to effectively assess the impact of your training in order to be able to keep moving forward, build on your success and overcome your problems. Developing a successful partnership that can consistently deliver outstanding ITE while still having its own unique characteristics is, without any doubt, a great challenge but is also hugely rewarding.

REFLECTIONS ON **CRITICAL ISSUES**

- *An ethos of high aspiration comes primarily from the leadership of the partnership and must be reinforced here and shared by all stakeholders.*
- *To build an effective learning community every partner must feel that they have an equal share and equal responsibility for the success of the partnership.*
- *Developing student teachers who are reflective practitioners requires mentors who are adept at this skill and can model and mentor effectively.*
- *The absence of an HEI partner in this school-centred model could draw criticism because of the perceived lack of research underpinning the*

programme. It is therefore important to instil in your trainees the value of scholarly activity to enhance the quality of their teaching and the development of their careers. This can be done in a number of ways including incorporation of enquiry-based learning within the programme. In an expansive learning environment the research and scholarship elements are modelled by many colleagues and practitioners at different stages in their careers, some of whom already have substantial academic qualifications while others are in the process of researching for their master's degrees while they are employed in school. The indirect influence of HEI contribution to teacher education cannot be underestimated.

- *Evaluating the impact of teacher education requires effective QA mechanisms that provide data, underpinned by enquiry and analysis of the 'story' behind the data to inform future improvement planning and to measure progress.*

| WHAT CAN WE LEARN FROM THE SHIFT TOWARDS A MORE SCHOOL-CENTRED MODEL IN THE NETHERLANDS?

Corinne van Velzen and Miranda Timmermans

CRITICAL **ISSUES**

- *Teacher education at school: who are the teacher educators?*
- *How do school–university partnerships facilitate learning opportunities for student teachers?*
- *How a work-based pedagogy in teacher education might look.*
- *Changing roles of teachers educators in school.*

Being a teacher educator in the Netherlands: a short overview

In the Netherlands several routes are open to those who want to become a teacher.

Case study

On completion of secondary education students can study at a university of applied sciences to become a teacher in primary or lower secondary (general and vocational) education through a four-year course. Subject knowledge and teaching knowledge are at the core of the curriculum.

To teach in higher secondary and pre-university education students must initially achieve a master's degree in a research university, following which they can enrol in a one-year post university course especially aimed at teaching aspects related to their subject. Students with a Bachelor's degree can apply for a master's course at a university of applied sciences and after graduation can teach in upper secondary education.

These routes share an important characteristic: the education of the student teacher is firmly founded in a TEI (either at a research university or a university of applied sciences) and in school experience. All routes can be characterised as practical and school-based, meaning the concerns, problems and dilemmas of school teachers are at the core of the curriculum and school experience plays an important role in teacher education. Korthagen and his colleagues (Korthagen et al, 2001) named this *realistic teacher education*. As a result, both at the institute and at school, professional guidance must be provided and teacher educators can be found in both institutions.

IBTEs work within the higher education context:

» providing student teachers with formal knowledge about teaching;

» supporting student teachers in reflecting on their practical experiences;

» discussing their development as a teacher centred on their portfolio of evidence.

In the Netherlands IBTEs do not have research obligations although some of them are involved in practical research or self-study projects. These teacher educators are seen as second-order teachers; that is, teachers of teachers rather than teachers of pupils (Murray and Male, 2005; Swennen, Chapter 2) and they are working in a second-order context (i.e. the institute rather than a school).

To understand the role and position of teacher educators at school (who are second-order teachers in the first-order context of the school) we have to take a look at the two ways school experiences in the Netherlands are organised. Most students still experience a traditional situation where the school and institute hardly work together. In this case a cooperating teacher (mentor) is responsible for emotional support, along with some coaching and feedback based on lesson observation. These cooperating teachers are not acknowledged as teacher educators. Some students (about 20%) are educated in School-University Partnerships in Teacher Education which started to evolve in the early years of this century inspired by similar developments in England (like the Oxford Internship Model, Benton (1990)) and the United States (especially the emergence of Professional Development Schools, Holmes-Partnership (2006)). School-university collaboration is based on formal agreements, and both the institute and school are responsible for the education and assessment of student teachers. To realise this, a shared vision of teacher education and a shared curriculum are needed, along with a shared quality assurance system. Most partnerships consist of several TEIs and schools.

Over the years, two types of cooperating teachers have developed in these schools. The first one is called a SBTE. These are acknowledged as teacher educators and they have to meet the same professional standards as their colleagues at the institute. They are responsible for:

» the coordination of the professional development of teachers in their school;

» the overall guidance of student teachers;

» maintaining the link with the TEIs.

The second kind of cooperating teachers at school are the traditional teacher mentors, generally experienced teachers and, in secondary education, teaching the same subject as the student teacher. They are responsible for the daily supervision of the student teacher. As a rule, mentors have had some training in coaching, observation and providing feedback. Until now, in the Netherlands, mentors have not been seen as teacher educators but we have found that they actually can act as teacher educators, while being a teacher, when they are guiding student teachers (van Velzen 2013). IBTEs work alongside SBTEs in schools on a regular but not full-time basis.

Critical question

» What challenges do your teachers face when taking on the role of teacher educator?

The roles of teacher educators in school

In school-university partnerships the school policy enables student teachers to experience being part of the school community as 'colleagues' rather than guests. They are able increasingly to participate in some of the practices, which is seen as legitimate peripheral participation in the social practice of the school (Lave and Wenger, 1991; Ragonis and Hazzan, 2009). Cooperating teachers provide guidance to support the student teachers and facilitate opportunities to observe in the classroom. An important prerequisite at school level to realise this peripherality is the 'safety net' built by the school to avoid putting pupil learning at risk.

Another aspect of the work of cooperating teachers is opening up the social context of the school for their novice colleagues. Student teachers are not only introduced to school life but they are entitled to participate in all teaching and teacher-related activities, supported by the SBTE and the mentor. For instance:

» they attend staff meetings about grading pupils or new teaching techniques;

» assessments are prepared together;

» the regular talks with parents about individual pupils are observed;

» student teachers are also involved in all extra-curricular activities like school camps, parties and even redesigning the teaching spaces.

The most important aspect, however, is the daily guidance of learning how to act and think as a teacher, working with pupils and the school curriculum. This being work-based learning, different pedagogical approaches are required than those used at the institute.

Three important features of a pedagogy of work-based teacher education can be identified, based on the ideas of Billett (2001):

1. the affordance (or invitational quality) of the school, which is facilitated by seeing student teachers as colleagues, opening up all teaching activities for student teachers and having a clear policy for initial teacher education;

2. the agency of student teachers; that is, their individual abilities and willingness to participate in school and to be supervised;

3. structure aimed at integrating theory and practice:

a. during actual teaching, to support the student teacher in learning to think and act as a teacher in a particular context;

b. after teaching, or other school experience, to aid the student teacher in rethinking knowledge needed to act in new situations and other contexts.

To achieve the above, in partner schools support is given by the SBTE and/or the mentor depending on the kind of activities. Of course it is important to remember that working this way is rather new for all the stakeholders. In practice the stories are sometimes less attractive. In the example, based on the research of Timmermans (2012), we show that the affordance of these partner schools is still based on the individual decisions of mentors instead of on shared views regarding the education of student teachers. Consequently, the extent of peripheral participation in teacher-related activities varies.

The affordance of partner schools in primary teacher education

Four types of activities are available for student teachers at school:

1. activities with or for pupils; for example planning, teaching and assessment;

2. activities at school level; for example communicating with parents, colleagues and other professionals;

3. accessibility and use of school-based resources; for example pupil files, school data, intranet and staff library.

4. activities aimed at teacher professional development; for example staff professional learning opportunities and feedback talks with the mentor.

Individual mentors, even within schools, differed considerably in which activities they asked of student teachers, which activities they allowed them to do and which activities were not available.

Research showed that:

» most activities were related to working with pupils and the use of school-based resources;

» more activities were allowed during the final year in which student teachers were enrolled in the teacher education course, probably based on ideas and convictions of mentors derived from their traditional practical experience;

» overall student teachers did not get the opportunity to practise all activities because not all possible activities were afforded or allowed over the four years of study;

» in the first three years most activities were voluntary. In the last year activities became mandatory, expecting the students to perform as teachers already;

» there was no sign that mentors provided activities related to the learning needs of the individual student teachers;

» the implicit ideas of individual mentors determined the work-based curriculum of the student teachers, instead of the content and rhythm of the work itself, which is characteristic for work-based learning.

(Timmermans, 2012)

Critical question

» What learning opportunities do your partner schools really afford to your student teachers?

Mentors: teacher educators modelling their teaching

All Dutch student teachers are supervised by a mentor in daily practice, although in different ways and with different aims. Mentors provide their student teachers with opportunities to experience teaching and support them emotionally in the process of learning to know what it means to become a teacher and to develop the self-esteem needed.

The practical knowledge of the experienced teachers acting as mentors 'encapsulates the essence of being an accomplished practitioner' (Loughran, 2010, p ix). Deconstructing this knowledge and sharing it with student teachers is seen as important because it can:

» prevent each individual student teacher from feeling pressured to 'reinvent the wheel' (Loughran, 2010);

» help to overcome the limitations of learning through observation alone (Lortie, 1975);

» be a tool for learning and instructional decision-making (Little, 2007);

» contribute to student teachers becoming knowledgeable professionals (Thiessen, 2000).

Making practical knowledge explicit is not easy, so the collaborative mentoring approach (below) was developed to help mentor teachers (a) to show experienced teacher behaviour and critically discuss this with student teachers (a process we called work-based modelling) and (b) to support the student teacher during actual teaching (by modelling – mentor behaving as teacher, and scaffolding – mentor behaving as a teacher educator).

The collaborative mentoring approach

This approach consists of cycles of lessons that are collaboratively prepared and evaluated by a student teacher and a mentor. The focus of discussions is the learning needs of the student teacher, but of course other issues can be discussed. The first lesson in the cycle is taught by the mentor. They model experienced teacher behaviour relevant to the learning needs of the student teacher. If, for example, the student teacher's focus is related to motivating the pupils, the mentor demonstrates this as clearly as possible. The third lesson will be taught by the student teacher, employing this teaching strategy, while the second lesson is co-taught by both teachers. Co-teaching means they are not just dividing tasks but each is responsible for the whole lesson (Roth and Tobin, 2002). Before the actual teaching starts agreements are made about signs teachers can give to each other when the student teacher wants help or the mentor wants to provide support. By intervening the mentor can address pupils and complete student teachers' statements or ask additional questions. In the interventions the mentor takes the teacher role (modelling) and the student teacher observes. The student teacher can then imitate the behaviour of the mentor, exploring whether this behaviour also works for them. If a lesson stalls, the mentor can step in and provide the student teacher with (whispered) hints and brief suggestions (scaffolding). Subsequently the student teacher continues the lesson.

Modelling and scaffolding practical knowledge

Mentoring conversations about modelling and scaffolding practical knowledge may include:
»   telling about teacher behaviour or ideas;

»   explaining one's own behaviour or ideas;

»   discussing the effectiveness of lesson plans;

»   discussing observations of lesson enactment by the mentor or student teacher;

»   discussing alternatives: reframing the situation and/or teachers' behaviour;

»   providing suggestions and discussing the expected effectiveness of these;

»   asking student teachers' suggestions and discussing the expected effectiveness of these;

»   giving feedback underpinned with vocational expertise;

»   comparing and discussing reflections written by the student teacher and the mentor.

Ways of modelling and scaffolding practical knowledge while teaching a co-taught lesson include:
»   demonstrating experienced teaching behaviour by the mentor;

»   stepping in, taking a teacher's role, and showing experienced teacher behaviour, which the student teacher observes and may imitate (modelling);

»   stepping in, taking a teacher educator's role, and making short statements or leading brief discussion on how to continue a lesson (scaffolding).

(Van Velzen, 2013)

Depending on the needs of the student teacher more than one lesson can be taught by the mentor or can be co-taught. At the same time the student teacher may have their own classes to teach where they continue to develop new teaching strategies. One can understand it is not an easy task for mentors to make the transition between the roles of teacher and teacher educator. Finding the right way (either as a teacher or as a teacher educator) and the right moment to intervene is one of the challenges mentors have to face.

Last, but not least, cooperating teachers should support student teachers while performing practical inquiries related to the improvement of their practice. All student teachers must perform such inquiries in their schools. Usually IBTEs provide this support; however, in partner schools this is a new role for cooperating teachers. Practical inquiry in these schools is not only a learning strategy for student teachers but also an important tool for school development. At the moment this role is seen as challenging and in most schools only a few teachers are able and willing to provide this support; alongside their student teachers they are pioneers in school-based inquiry. In Chapter 4 (Roberts) there are practical ideas to support teacher educators in undertaking this extended role.

Providing social and emotional support and the development of self-esteem, sharing practical knowledge and performing practical inquiries are the three important facets of mentoring student teachers (Wang and Odell, 2002). Each of them places unique demands on the mentors, and choosing when a specific approach is required is an important aspect of their professionalism.

Critical questions

» How are you enabling your mentors to develop their pedagogical approaches?

» Are you fully utilising the opportunities that exist for work-based learning in your context?

IN A **NUTSHELL**

The assumption that student teachers must be educated at schools and at TEIs and that schools and universities must collaborate in order to provide student teachers with the best from both worlds underpins school-university partnerships. In practice, however, this is not always easy to realise. The learning opportunities that are needed for educating student teachers are broadly acknowledged within partner schools although they are not always recognisable in daily practice. SBTEs are frequently in contact with their colleagues at the institute and, more specifically, with the IBTE placed at school. As an outcome of this collaboration these school mentors are less isolated than those in more traditional school contexts. Clearer leadership by the school management, however, would be helpful, as shown in the example of Timmermans (2012).

REFLECTIONS ON **CRITICAL ISSUES**

- *As a result of the growing responsibility of schools for the education of student teachers we need a work-based pedagogy.*
- *The guidance that cooperating mentors provide is an important aspect of such pedagogy.*
- *The acknowledgement of mentors being teacher educators in actual practice is still somewhat controversial even among mentors themselves. Emotional support and supporting self-esteem is a well-known aspect of a pedagogy of work-based teacher education, but sharing practical knowledge, co-teaching and intervening in the lesson enactment of the student teacher is less known, though seen as important and helpful.*
- *New learning arrangements (both formal and at the workplace) have to be developed for mentors in order to support the expansion of the competences needed.*
- *Supervising practical inquiries is seen as even more difficult. It is helpful when teachers themselves start to systematically question their own practice, but until now this is not standard practice.*
- *At the moment, a lot of cooperating mentors do not experience these activities as 'teacher educator' or 'researcher' as part of their profession, let alone of their identity. Becoming second-order teachers in a first-order context indeed is hard, and changing these convictions is one of the most important challenges in work-based teacher education we have to face right now.*

REFERENCES

Alexander, R J (ed) (2010) *Children, Their World, Their Education – Final Report and Recommendations of the Cambridge Primary Review.* Abingdon: Routledge.

Bass, B M and Avolio, B J (1993) Transformational leadership and organizational culture. *Public Administration Quarterly*, 17: 112–21.

Bates, T, Swennen, A and Jones, K (2011) *The Professional Development of Teacher Educators.* Abingdon, Routledge.

Beauchamp, C and Thomas, L (2009) Understanding teacher identity: an overview of issues in the literature and implications for teacher education. *Cambridge Journal of Education*, 39: 175–89.

Beijaard, D, Meijer, P and Verloop, N (2004) Reconsidering research on teachers' professional identity. *Teaching and Teacher Education*, 20: 107–28.

Bell, M and Cordingley, P (2014) *Characteristics of High Performing Schools – Teach First Research Report.* Coventry: CUREE Ltd.

Benton, P (1990) *The Oxford Internship Scheme: Integration and Partnership in Initial Teacher Education.* London: Calouste Gulbenkian Foundation.

BERA-RSA (2014) Research and the teaching profession – building capacity for a self-improving education system. London: BERA. Available at: www.bera.ac.uk/project/research-and-teacher-education [accessed 5 August 2014].

Berliner, D C (2001) Learning about and learning from expert teachers. *International Journal of Educational Research*, 35, 463–82.

Berry, A (2009). Professional self-understanding as expertise in teaching about teaching. *Teachers and Teaching: Theory and Practice*, 15: 305–18.

Billett, S (2001) Co-participation: affordance and engagement at work. *New Directions for Adult and Continuing Education. Special issue: Socio-Cultural Perspectives on Learning through Work*, 92: 63–72.

Bolam, R, McMahon, A, Stoll, L, Thomas, S and Wallace, M (2005) *Creating and Sustaining Effective Professional Learning Communities.* London: DfES.

Boyd, P and Harris, K (2010) Becoming a university lecturer in teacher education: expert school teachers reconstructing their pedagogy and identity. *Professional Development in Education*, 36: 9–24.

Boyer, E L (1990) *Scholarship Reconsidered: Priorities of the Professoriate.* Princeton, NJ: Princeton University Press.

Brew, A and Boud, D (1995) Teaching and Research: Establishing the Vital Link with Learning. *Higher Education*, 29: 261–73.

Brubaker, R and Cooper, F (2000) Beyond identity. *Theory and Society*, 29: 1–47.

Cheng, M M H, Tang, S Y F and Cheng, A Y N (2012) Practicalising theoretical knowledge in student teachers' professional learning in initial teacher education. *Teaching and Teacher Education*, 28: 781–90.

Chetty, R and Lubben, F (2010) The scholarship of research in teacher education in a higher education institution in transition: issues of identity. *Teaching and Teacher Education*, 26: 813–20.

Cochran-Smith, M (2003) Learning and unlearning: the education of teacher educators. *Teaching and Teacher Education*, 19: 5–28.

Cochran-Smith, M (2005) Teacher educators as researchers: multiple persectives. *Teaching and Teacher Education*, 21, 219–25.

Cochran-Smith, M and Lytle, S L (2009) *Inquiry as Stance: Practitioner Research for the Next Generation*. New York: Teachers College Press.

Cooperrider, D L and Whitney, D (2005) *A Positive Revolution in Change: Appreciative Inquiry*. San Francisco: Berrett-Koehler.

Costa, A L and Kallick, B (1993) Through the eyes of a critical friend. *Educational Leadership*, 51: 49–51.

Davey, R (2013) *The Professional Identity of Teacher Educators. Career on the Cusp?* Abingdon: Routledge.

Day, C and Harris, A (2002) Teacher leadership, reflective practice, and school improvement. *Second International Handbook of Educational Leadership and Administration*. Netherlands: Springer.

DfE (2010) The Importance of Teaching: Schools White Paper. London: The Stationery Office.

DfE (2011) Training our next generation of outstanding teachers. Available at: https://www.gov.uk/government/publications/training-our-next-generation-of-outstanding-teachers-an-improvement-strategy-for-discussion [accessed 28 May 2014].

DfE (2012a) *Teaching schools – background*. Available at: http://www.education.gov.uk/nationalcollege/index/support-for-schools/teachingschools/teachingschools-background.htm [accessed 29 October 2012].

DfE (2012b) Teachers' Standards. Available at: https://www.gov.uk/government/publications/teachers-standards [accessed 31 December 2013].

Dinkelman, T, Margolis, J and Sikkenga, K (2006) From teacher to teacher educator: experiences, expectations, and expatriation. *Studying Teacher Education*, 2: 5–23.

Ducharme, E (1993) *The Lives of Teacher Educators*. New York: Teachers College Press.

Eaude, T (2012) *How Do Expert Primary Classteachers Really Work? A Critical Guide for Teachers, Headteachers and Teacher Educators*. Northwich: Critical Publishing.

ESRC (2006) Demographic Review of the Social Sciences. Swindon: ESRC.

Feather, D (2010) A whisper of academic identity: an HE in FE perspective. *Research in Post-Compulsory Education*, 15: 189–204.

Field, S (2012) The trials of transition, and the impact upon the pedagogy of new teacher educators. *Professional Development in Education*, 38: 811–26.

Fisher, A, Russell, K, Macblain, S, Purdy, N, Curry, A and Macblain, A (2010) Re-examining the culture of learning in ITE: engaging with the new demands of the 21st century. *Critical and Reflective Practice in Education*, 2: 92–102.

Fisher, R L (2009) Who is a teacher educator?, in Klecka, C L, Odell, S J, Houston, W R and Mcbee, R H (eds) *Vision for Teacher Educators: Perspectives on the Association of Teacher Educators' Standards*. Lanham: Rowman and Littlefield Education.

Furlong, J, Barton, L, Miles, S, Whiting, C and Whitty, G (2000) *Teacher Education in Transition. Reforming Professionalism?* Buckingham: Open University Press.

Goldacre, B (2013) Building evidence into education. Available at: http://www.bera.ac.uk/resources/dfe-review-evidence-education-0 [accessed 28 October 2013].

Hargreaves, D (1996) *Teaching as a Research-Based Profession: Possibilities and Prospects*. London: Teacher Training Agency (TTA). Annual Lecture.

Harrison, J and Mckeon, F (2008) The formal and situated learning of beginning teacher educators in England: identifying characteristics for successful induction in the transition from workplace in schools to workplace in higher education. *European Journal of Teacher Education*, 31: 151–68.

Hermans, H and Hermans-Konopka, A (2010) *Dialogical Self Theory: Positioning and Counter-Positioning in a Globalizing Society*. Cambridge: Cambridge University Press.

Hodgkinson, H and Hodgkinson, P (2005) Improving schoolteachers' workplace learning. *Research Papers in Education*, 20: 109–31.

Holmes-Partnership (2006) *The Holmes Partnership Trilogy: Tomorrow's Teachers, Tomorrow's Schools, Tomorrow's Schools of Education*. New York: Peter Lang Publishing.

Hoyle, E (1975) Professionality, Professionalism and Control in Teaching, in Houghton, V, McHugh, R and Morgan, C (eds) *Management in Education. Reader 1: The Management of Organisations and Individuals*. London: Ward Lock Educational in association with Open University Press.

Hughes, M (ed) (2005). *The Mythology of Research and Teaching Relationships in Universities*. Maidenhead: SRHE and Open University.

Jarvis, J (2013) Becoming a teacher educator: developing a new aspect to your identity, in White, E and Jarvis, J (eds) *School-Based Teacher Training: A Handbook for Tutors and Mentors*. London: Sage.

Jarvis, J and White, E (2013). The pedagogy of teacher educators, in White, E and Jarvis, J (eds) *School-Based Teacher Training: A handbook for Tutors and Mentors*. London: Sage.

Jenkins, R (1996) *Social Identity*. London: Routledge.

Kamler, B (2008) Rethinking doctoral publication practices: writing from and beyond the thesis. *Studies in Higher Education*, 33: 283–94.

Kane, R (2003) Essay review. *Teaching and Teacher Education*, 19: 371–75.

Klecka, C L, Donovan, L, Venditti, K J and Short, B (2008) Who is a teacher educator? Enactment of teacher educator identity through electronic portfolio development. *Action in Teacher Education*, 29: 83–91.

Korthagen, F, Loughran, J and Russell, T (2006) Developing fundamental principles for teacher education programs and practices. *Teaching and Teacher Education*, 22: 1020–41.

Korthagen, F A J (2004) In search of the essence of a good teacher: towards a more holistic approach in teacher education. *Teaching and Teacher Education*, 20: 77–97.

Korthagen, F A J, Kessels, J P A M, Koster, B, Lagerwerf, B and Wubbels, T (2001) *Linking Practice and Theory: The Pedagogy of Realistic Teacher Education*. Mahwah, New Jersey: Laurence Erlbaum.

Korthagen, F A J, Loughran, J and Lunenberg, M (2005) Teaching teachers: studies into the expertise of teacher educators. *Teaching and Teacher Education*, 21: 107–15.

Kosnik, C (2007) Still the same yet different: Enduring values and commitments in my work as a teacher and teacher educator, in Russell, T and Loughran, J (eds) *Enacting a Pedagogy of Teacher Education: Values, Relationships and Practices*. London/New York: Routledge.

Lamont, M (1992) *Money, Morals, and Manners: the Culture of the French and the American Upper-Middle Class*. Chicago: University of Chicago Press.

Lampert, M (2010) Learning Teaching in, from, and for Practice: What Do We Mean? *Journal of Teacher Education*, 61: 21–34.

Lave, J and Wenger, E (1991) *Situated Learning: Legitimate Peripheral Participation*. Cambridge: Cambridge University Press.

Lewis, S, Passmore, J and Cantori, S (2011) *Appreciative Inquiry for Change Management: Using Appreciative Inquiry to Facilitate Organisational Development*. London: Kogan Press.

Little, J W (2007) *Teacher's Account of Classroom Experience as a Resource for Professional Learning and Instructional Decision Making*. Oxford: Blackwell Publishing.

Lortie, D C (1975) *Schoolteacher: A Sociological Study*. Chicago: The Chicago University Press.

Loughran, J (2006) *Developing a Pedagogy of Teacher Education: Understanding Teaching and Learning about Teaching*. London: Routledge.

Loughran, J (2010) *What Expert Teachers Do: Enhancing Professional Knowledge for Classroom Practice*. London: Routledge.

Maguire, M (2000) Inside/outside the ivory tower: teacher education in the English academy. *Teaching in Higher Education*, 5: 149–65.

McDrury, M and Alterio, J (2003) *Learning Through Storytelling in Higher Education: Using Reflection and Experience to Improve Learning*. London: Kogan Press.

Murray, J (2002) Between the chalkface and the ivory towers? A study of the professionalism of teacher educators working on primary initial teacher education courses in the English university sector. PhD, University of London.

Murray, J (2006) Investigating good practices in the induction of teacher educators into Higher Education. Available at: http://escalate.ac.uk/1149 [accessed 13 October 2011].

Murray, J, Campbell, A, Hextall, I, Hulme, M, Jones, M, Mahony, P, Menter, I, Procter, R and Wall, K (2009) Research and teacher education in the UK: building capacity. *Teaching and Teacher Education*, 25, 944–50.

Murray, J and Male, T (2005) Becoming a teacher educator: evidence from the field. *Teaching and Teacher Education*, 21, 125–42.

Penuel, W and Wertsch, J (1995) Vygotsky and identity formation: a sociocultural approach. *Educational Psychologist*, 30, 83–92.

Ragonis, N and Hazzan, O (2009) A tutoring model for promoting the pedagogical-disciplinary skills of prospective teachers. *Mentoring & Tutoring: Partnership in Learning*, 17: 67–82.

Roth, W-M and Tobin, K (2002) *At the Elbow of Another: Learning to Teach by Coteaching*. New York: Peter Lang.

Savin-Baden, M (2008) *Learning Spaces*. Berkshire: Open University Press.

Schön, D A (2003) *The Reflective Practitioner: How Professionals Think in Action*. Aldershot: Ashgate.

Seel, R (2008) Introduction to appreciative inquiry. Available at: http://www.new-paradigm.co.uk/introduction_to_ai.htm [accessed 4 April 2013].

Shulman, L (2005) The signature pedagogies of the professions of law, medicine, engineering and the clergy: potential lessons for the education of teachers. *The Math Science Partnerships Workshop 'Teacher Education for Effective Teaching and Learning'*. Available at: http://www.taylorprograms.com/images/Shulman_Signature_Pedagogies.pdf [accessed 5 August 2014].

Snoek, M, Swennen A and Klink M V D (2011) The quality of teacher educators in the European policy debate: actions and measures to improve the professionalism of teacher educators. *Professional Development in Education*, 37: 651–64.

Stenhouse, L (1975) *An Introduction to Curriculum Research and Development*. London: Heineman.

Swennen, A (2012) Van oppermeesters tot docenten hoger onderwijs: De ontwikkeling van het beroep en de identiteit van lerarenopleiders [The development of the profession and identity of teacher educators]. Amsterdam: VU University Amsterdam.

Swennen, A, Lunenberg, M and Korthagen, F (2008) Preach what you teach! Teacher educators and congruent teaching. *Teachers and Teaching: Theory and Practice*, 14 (5): 531–42.

Swennen, A, Shagrir, L and Cooper, M (2009) Becoming a teacher educator: voices of beginning teacher educators, in Swennen, A and Van Der Klink, M (eds) *Becoming a Teacher Educator: Theory and Practice for Teacher Educators*. Dordrecht: Springer.

Taylor, A (2008) Developing understanding about learning to teach in a university-schools partnership in England. *British Educational Research Journal*, 34: 63–90.

Teaching Agency (2012) A guide to school direct 2013–14. Available at: http://webarchive.nationalarchives. gov.uk/20130401151715/https://www.education.gov.uk/publications/eOrderingDownload/Guide%20to%20 School%20Direct%202013–14.pdf [accessed 28 May 2014].

Thiessen, D (2000) A skillful start to a teaching career: a matter of developing impactful behaviours, reflective practices, or professional knowledge? *International Journal of Educational Research*, 33: 515–37.

Timmermans, M (2012) Kwaliteit van de opleidingsschool. Over affordance, agency en competentieontwikkeling [Quality of the opleidingsschool on affordance, agency and competence development]. Doctoral Dissertation, Tilburg University, the Netherlands.

Timperley, H, Wilson, A, Barrar, H and Fung, I (2007) Teacher professional learning and development: Best evidence synthesis iteration [BES]. Available at: http://www.educationcounts.govt.nz/publications/ series/2515/15341 [accessed 28 October 2013].

Troman, G (1996) Models of the 'good' teacher: defining and redefining teacher quality, in Woods, P (ed) *Contemporary Issues in Teaching and Learning*. London: Routledge.

Ure, C L (2010) Reforming teacher education through a professionally applied study of teaching. *Journal of Education for Teaching*, 36: 461–75.

van Velzen, C (2013) Guiding learning teaching. PhD, Vrije Universiteit.

van Velzen, C, van Der Klink, M, Swennen, A and Yaffe, E (2010) The induction and needs of beginning teacher educators. *Professional Development in Education*, 36: 61–75.

van Velzen, C, Volman, M, Brekelmans, M and White, S (2012) Guided work-based learning: sharing practical teaching knowledge with student teachers. *Teaching and Teacher Education*, 28: 229–39.

Wang, J and Odell, S J (2002) Mentored learning to teach according to standards-based reform: a critical review. *Review of Educational Research*, 72: 481–546.

White, E (2014) Being a teacher and a teacher educator – developing a new identity? *Professional Development in Education*, 40(3): 436–49.

White, E and Jarvis, J (eds) (2013) *School-Based Teacher Training. A Handbook for Tutors and Mentors*. London: Sage.

White, E, Roberts, A, Rees, M and Read, M (2013) An exploration of the development of academic identity in a School of Education. *Professional Development in Education*, 40: 56–70.

Zeichner, K (1995) Beyond the divide of teacher research and academic research. *Teachers and Teaching: Theory and Practice*, 1, 153–72.

Zeichner, K (2005a) Becoming a teacher educator: a personal perspective. *Teaching and Teacher Education*, 21: 117–24.

Zeichner, K (2005b) A research agenda for teacher education, in Cochran-Smith, M and Zeichner, K (eds) *Studying Teacher Education*. New Jersey: Lawrence Erlbaum and the American Educational Research Association.

Zeichner, K (2005c) Research on teacher thinking and different views of reflective practice in teaching and teacher education, in Handal, G and Vaage, S (eds) *Teachers' Minds and Actions: Research on Teachers' Thinking and Practice*. Routledge.

Zeichner, K (2010) Rethinking the connections between campus courses and field experiences in college- and university-based teacher education. *Journal of Teacher Education*, 61: 89–99.

Zeichner, K and Gore, J (1990) Teacher socialization, in Houston, W R (ed) *Handbook of Research on Teacher Education: A Project of the Association of Teacher Educators*. New York: MacMillan.

INDEX